FRESHWATER FISHING

EDITED BY
STEVE STARLING

BayBooks
An imprint of HarperCollins*Publishers*

CONTENTS

A BAY BOOKS PUBLICATION
An imprint of HarperCollinsPublishers

First published in Australia in 1993 by Bay Books, of
CollinsAngus&Robertson Publishers Pty Limited (ACN 009 913 517)
A division of HarperCollinsPublishers (Australia) Pty Limited
25 Ryde Road, Pymble NSW 2073, Australia

HarperCollinsPublishers (New Zealand) Limited
31 View Road, Glenfield, Auckland 10, New Zealand

HarperCollinsPublishers Limited
77– 85 Fulham Palace Road, London W6 8JB, United Kingdom

Copyright © Bay Books 1993

National Library of Australia
Cataloguing-in-Publication data:

Freshwater fishing.
ISBN 1 86378 109 9.

1. Fishing – Australia – Guidebooks. 2 Freshwater fishes – Australia.
I. Starling, Stephen. (Series: Fishing Australia).
799.120994

Printed in Singapore
Cover Photograph: Fishing for red fin in a Lachlan billabong, NSW.

5 4 3 2 1
97 96 95 94 93

CONTRIBUTORS

The publisher gratefully acknowledges the assistance of
the many contributors to Fishing Australia

Editor
Steve Starling

Assistant Editor
Dave Lockwood

Writers and Photographers
Paul Barker, Glen Booth, Bill Classon, Gene Dundon, Sean
Fitzgerald, Ashley Hallam, Mark Hanlon, Peter Horrobin, Alex
Julius, Dave Lockwood, Lawrie and Julie McEnally, Shane
Mensforth, Dave Roche, Gavin Ryan, Steve Starling, Warren
Steptoe, Nic van Oudtshoorn, Mary Jo Wilson

Artists
Greg Gaul, Kevan Hardacre, Gerry Murphy

INTRODUCTION

It's ironic that, while Australia is rated as the second driest continent on earth (after Antarctica), freshwater angling is without doubt our fastest growing form of recreational fishing!

Freshwater fishing emerged from virtual obscurity during the 1960s and 1970s, to become the most exciting and dynamic sector of the entire sport in the '80s. In the 1990s, Australian freshwater angling is undergoing a period of consolidation and refinement. It stands proudly alongside its various saltwater counterparts in terms of the sophistication of its tackle and techniques, not to mention the dedication and commitment of its many keen practitioners.

In all its diverse forms — from bait soaking and lure tossing to trolling and fly casting — Australian freshwater fishing can truly be said to have come of age. It has borrowed tackle and tactics from around the world and added uniquely Australian twists to most of them. Today, the sport supports a quarterly, full-colour magazine, as well as several one-off titles and books each year, and also accounts for as much as a third of the content of our regular angling publications. Furthermore, an increasing number of instructional videos and television fishing shows are now devoted to inland angling in its many forms.

The appeal of freshwater fishing is obvious to most who give it a go. The mix of challenge, thrill and reward are just about perfect for many people. As an added bonus, the sport is undertaken in some of the country's most delightful environments; from casuarina-lined bass pools on our coastal rivers, to vast outback dams and sparkling high country troutstreams.

Best of all, freshwater fishing is more easily accessible in Australia than just about anywhere else on earth! Sport that would cost a fortune to enjoy in Europe, or attract dense crowds of hopeful anglers in North America, is absolutely free and largely under-utilised in this country.

Almost all our waters are public, and apart from some sensible angling restrictions and a few grey areas in our private property and riparian access laws, there is little to stop the average man, woman or child from fishing where he or she wishes. This is a uniquely privileged situation which too many of us take for granted.

Of course, to reciprocate for this free and easy access, all freshwater anglers need to steadfastly defend and protect the resources which provide their sport.

While the future outlook for freshwater fishing is bright in many areas — particularly the widespread stocking of artificial impoundments — other inland angling environments and fish populations are under dire pressure. In particular, our outback and coastal rivers have been seriously degraded through poor farming and land management practices, along with the construction of major barriers to fish migration and reproduction in the form of dams, weirs and barrages. Throw in the spread of noxious, exotic fish species, over-harvesting by commercial and amateur fishermen and the increasing frequency of toxic algal blooms and the overall picture takes on a sombre hue.

Thankfully, these forms of environmental and biological degradation are now widely recognised. In a few instances at least, meaningful remedial works are in progress, and many more are planned. Also, it seems unlikely that future enemies of the aquatic world will enjoy the same free hand to plunder and pillage as they did during the darkest days of rampant (and unsustainable) development that occurred over the last three decades. There's a long way to go in many areas, but we have cause for a reasonable level of optimism about the longterm future of our freshwater fisheries.

Meanwhile, there are few better ways of spending a day or a week than casting a line into one of our many sweetwater streams and lakes. Freshwater angling is truly a thinking person's recreation, and the study of its forms can provide a lifetime of pleasure ... The pages of this excellent new publication are as fine a place to start that lifetime of learning as any!

Steve Starling

BETTER FISHING

All successful anglers must first understand, and then build upon the basics. This section shows how and when to fish, where to find fish, and how to master freshwater fishing techniques such as fly fishing, trolling and fishing with lures. There are also guides to trout tactics and finding bass streams.

FRESHWATER FISHING

Exploring Inland Options

Australia is one of the driest continents on earth, yet despite this fact, freshwater fishing remains one of the country's most popular forms of angling.

Murray cod

Golden perch

Most enthusiastic Australian anglers have, at some stage, sampled the freshwater fishing on offer in this country. In New South Wales alone, nearly 100,000 freshwater fishing licences are sold every year, a figure which does not include youngsters, some pensioners, Aborigines and those people who risk a fine by not buying a licence. In reality, it's likely that almost 200,000 New South Welshmen wet a line in our rivers, lakes and dams every year!

For the vast majority of anglers, Australian freshwater fishing centres around the introduced brown and rainbow trout. Since the late 1800s, trout have thrived in alpine, sub-alpine and cool tableland regions of Australia, now inhabiting most southern lakes, large dams, rivers and adjoining creek systems.

But besides trout and other 'imports' such as redfin perch and carp, there are a wealth of challenging freshwater fish to be caught from Australia's southern inland river systems, dams and lakes.

This formidable range of native freshwater fish provides a great challenge for amateur anglers. Considering the diversity of environments in which freshwater fish can be caught in this country, and the typically Australian setting of most inland fishing spots, it's not at all surprising that freshwater fishing is so popular. In fact nearly every pocket of freshwater in Australia carries at least one variety of fish that can be caught using conventional angling methods.

CUTTING TIME WITH SPLIT RING PLIERS

If you're one of those lure tossers who invariably beefs-up lures with heavier duty hooks and split rings, a pair of split ring pliers can save a lot of time, effort and frustration, not to mention the inevitable cut fingers.

Split ring pliers have a toothed jaw that separates the ring and holds it open while pressure is being applied to the plier handles. Certain multi-purpose fishing pliers can also carry out this function as well as being useful for other fishing chores.

'Nearly every pocket of freshwater in Australia carries at least one variety of fish that can be caught using conventional angling methods.'

PREVIOUS PAGE: The mighty Murray cod — our largest freshwater sportfish.
ABOVE: Weirs such as this one on the Lachlan in NSW often provide great fishing.

'Golden perch, silver perch, Macquarie perch, eel-tail catfish and Murray cod are the most popular inland native species.'

Silver perch

Basically, there are two major divisions of Australian freshwater fishing. The most heavily fished is the southern freshwater scene, covering that area south of the Tropic of Capricorn.

Inland Natives

For years, Australian native freshwater fish have been victims of less than sporting fishing tactics. Once prolific, fish stocks were dramatically depleted by the use of heavy cord set lines, illegal nets and even dynamite!

Thankfully, sportfishing oriented amateur anglers have helped to limit such activities and to educate the public about our wonderful natives. Today, the full potential of this unique freshwater fishery is finally being realised.

Lure casting and fly fishing — techniques not at all dissimiliar to traditional trout catching methods — have proven extremely productive and exciting ways to catch our native fish. Light to medium spinning outfits employing line between 2 and 8 kg breaking strain offer a challenging combination for catching all these natives, up to and including the mighty Murray cod.

Most inland lake and river systems which hold stocks of native fish can be actively fished from the shore, from a canoe or small dinghy. The best fishing spots in these systems are usually those well off the beaten track, found only by the more adventurous anglers.

Golden perch, silver perch, Macquarie perch, eel-tail catfish and Murray cod are the most popular inland native species. The less common trout cod and freshwater blackfish are generally incidental angling captures, and these days fishermen are encouraged to release alive any trout cod and 'slipperies' they hook.

When and How to Fish

Peak fishing time for natives often revolves around high or rising barometric pressure and a rise in water temperature: trends generally associated with spring and early summer.

When cold water flows down from the higher alpine region during winter, native freshwater fish may become inactive and bait is often more effective than lures.

Mudeyes, shrimp, crayfish, worms, frogs and small fish (check local fisheries' restrictions), are a few of the most appealing baits for natives, while large woodgrubs, also known as bardi grubs, are still one of the top Murray cod takers in most areas.

BELOW: A big golden perch, also called yellowbelly or callop. These incredibly hardy native battlers inhabit a diverse range of outback habitats.

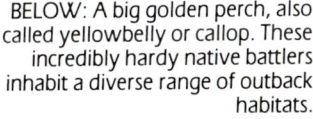

G. E. Schmida · A.N.T. Photo Library

Eel-tailed catfish

Q & A

What is one of the safest ways of storing terminal tackle?

Good quality terminal tackle is by no means cheap and, due to its size, is one of the easiest items of tackle to misplace. The best approach for storing terminals is to set aside a separate tackle box that fits inside your creel, basket or main tackle box. One small modification to these involves glueing angled pieces of plastic, aluminium strips or even vinyl into each compartment. This will ensure the delicate task of removing terminals from the tackle box is easier and safer.

ABOVE: A lovely kilo-plus Macquarie perch taken from Victoria's Dartmouth Dam on a 'high tech' computer baitcaster.
BELOW: The rare and endangered trout cod is now found in just a handful of localities.

Among the productive lure patterns are the spinning blade trout lures, small spoons, deep diving plugs and even surface lures, especially at night.

Finding congregations of native fish in a river or lake system requires locating fish holding structures such as a deep hole, rocky gorge, wood pile, undercut bank or sunken timber. Late afternoon, early morning and night fishing sessions will prove the most productive.

The areas immediately downstream of weirs and other obstructions are also worthy of special attention, particularly during a 'fresh' or rise in river height.

The Great Awakening

Despite the one-eyed attitude of some dedicated trout anglers, and the neglect of unscrupulous land developers, farmers and government bodies who have little regard for fish management, Australia's native freshwater fish are surviving and remain one of our most valuable angling assets.

While stocks of certain species have diminished, the bulk of Australian native freshwater fish are thriving in a wide range of inland river and lake systems. Sadly, this is more a testimony to the toughness and durability of the fish than to our record of management.

In recent years, amateur anglers, alarmed over the increasing scarcity of some native freshwater species, have banded together and formed protection societies and lobby groups aimed at saving our natives and educating people about their worth.

Many conservation minded anglers fish for Australian natives purely on a catch and release basis, or at least return the vast majority of their catch to the water alive. This trend is to be applauded and encouraged as the way of the future.

The Unwanted Immigrants

In these days of conservation and shrinking fish stocks, it may seem a little ironic that certain fisheries' rules and regulations actually demand that the fish you catch be killed and not returned to the water! Such is the case with the introduced carp and redfin (English perch). Even more ironic, this very law is a conservation act in itself!

G E Schmida A N T Photo Library

Wade Hughes / Lochman Transparencies

ABOVE: This redfin perch took a small leadhead jig worked close to the bottom in Drakes Brook Dam, near Waroona, W.A.
RIGHT: At 1.5 kg this Australian bass is significantly larger than average for the species.

'Carp put up a strong fight when hooked on light gear, though sadly most specimens from Australian waters are practically inedible.'

Although both of these introduced fish species provide good sport and an important fishery in some of our more heavily urbanised areas, and despite the fact that the redfin is particularly good eating, these two immigrant fish are a constant threat to our more valuable and vulnerable native fish populations.

European carp and, to a lesser extent, their relatives the goldfish, tench and roach, can choke a river system, carry disease and devour the young of native fish. The redfin has similar unpopular habits, and is a very avid destroyer of young fish, natives and trout.

Be that as it may, catching these so-called pests can be one of the most enjoyable forms of conservation imaginable!

The redfin or English perch inhabits inland dams, lakes and adjoining river systems in New South Wales, Victoria, parts of South Australia and the southern western corner of Western Australia. They provide good fishing for both the lure caster and the bait fisherman, from both shore and boats.

Redfin are commonly taken on worms, shrimps, yabbies and small live fish, while favoured lure patterns include spinners, spoons, small diving plugs and wet flies. They also respond very well to vertically jigged lures or 'bobbers'. When feeding at the surface, redfin are a challenging prospect for dry fly and nymph fishermen using light trout catching tackle.

Most redfin average between 200 grams and 1 kg, though some waters become over populated with tiny stunted reddies. At the opposite extreme, a few lakes and dams produce redfin in the 1 to 3 kg range on a fairly regular basis.

The Carp Curse

Carp are a different kettle of fish, having reached near plague proportions in many river systems of southern Australia.

Where anglers fish for other more desirable fish, carp are regarded as noxious pests,

Macquarie perch

though in some areas they do at least provide active sport for kids, novices and fish-starved anglers.

Most carp are caught using bread, dough, sweet corn, worms or pudding baits, though they will sometimes respond to small lures and present quite a challenge on nymphs fished off light fly tackle.

Carp put up a strong fight when hooked on light gear, though sadly most specimens from Australian waters are practically inedible unless doused with rich sauces or disguised with spices. Their flesh has been described as tasting like soap liberally laced with fine bones!

Bass As Australian As Vegemite!

The Australian bass (*Macquaria novemaculeata*), although yet another victim of poor river management, remains another of our great angling assets.

Bass were once found in nearly every coastal river and creek system from Southern Queensland to the Hopkins River in Western Victoria. Today they still fill this vast range, but many gaps exist in their distribution.

Inhabiting freshwater for the greater part of their lives, bass must migrate to brackish water to spawn, usually during late winter.

It is this migration that has led to problems with bass stocks, as the damming of many rivers, along with construction of smaller weirs, crossings and barrages has effectively prevented adult fish from running downstream to spawn or, worse still, stopped the tiny juveniles from travelling back up the rivers.

Nowadays, much smaller populations of bass exist than ever before. For this reason, most conservation minded anglers fish bass purely for enjoyment, and safeguard their pastime by ensuring all fish are handled carefully and returned to the water.

Catching Bass

Lure fishing is much preferred to soaking baits, not only because the fish are easier to release and less likely to be gut-hooked, but simply because bass love lures and provide exceptional action when taken that way.

Australian bass are extremely reliant on structures, rarely venturing far from cover unless concealed by the dark of night, or induced by an attractive lure.

They reside around sunken timber, rock ledges, undercut banks and below dams,

weirs, or water falls where their progress upriver has been halted.

The most effective bass fishing tackle consists of a light threadline or baitcasting (plug) reel mated to a 1.5 to 2 metre light-tipped casting rod.

As most bass today average around 500 grams in weight, and a top specimen rarely exceeds 2 kg, bass are usually fished for in a sporting manner with lines between 2 and 4 kg breaking strain.

During bright daylight hours, small deep-diving plugs that run close to holed-up bass are the most productive lure patterns.

Early in the morning, and especially at dusk and into the night, surface lures are a near sure bet for an exciting and rewarding fishing stint. Jitterbugs, Crazy Crawlers, Hula Poppers and Tiny Torpedoes are some of the more popular topwater patterns.

Fly rodders also find bass a willing target and large bushy-haired bass bugs and small popping flies secure the majority of hook-ups.

BELOW: Rugged up against the cold of an alpine autumn, this angler has taken four big trout; two rainbows and two browns.

ABOVE: Netting a brown trout taken on the troll in a high country lake. Trout respond to a variety of techniques ranging from bait fishing to fly casting.

'Trout tend to favour the food-rich shorelines and are commonly taken by shore anglers as well as boaties.'

Trout in Australia

Basically, there are two separate stocks of trout in Australia: those that are the offspring of wild, self-sustaining fish and those that are born in hatcheries and later released into inland impoundments or rivers for recreational angling purposes.

The two common trout species in Australia are the brown and the rainbow. Browns usually make their spawning run between May and July, while rainbows lay eggs a little later, from June through to October. Early spawning run trout that coincide with the tail-end of the fishing season can provide furious and exciting fishing for river anglers.

Throughout the rest of the year, trout are fairly regularly captured from inland impoundments, alpine river and adjoining creek systems. There's a general trend for lake trout to grow faster and reach a greater size than those fish which spend their lives within the stream or river networks.

Q & A

Can you catch freshwater fish at night?
Yes. Most species of native and introduced freshwater fish are active night feeders. Often the best bite will be found just after dusk and for the few hours following sunset. Trout are one species that are caught right through the hours of darkness. Bass, Murray cod, yellowbelly and catfish also feed freely at night.

In the lake environment, trout often congregate around prominent bottom structures such as sunken timber, underwater rocky outcrops and steep drop-offs. As the water warms up in summer these same lake fish, bound by water temperature, congregate near thermoclines — the layers of sudden change from warm to cool water.

Trout tend to favour the food-rich shorelines and are commonly taken by shore anglers as well as boaties. They have a particular affiliation with the shallows during spring and autumn when insect activity coincides with lower water temperatures. Fly fishermen relish these periods.

The trout's diet consists mainly of aquatic insects, terrestrial insects that breed or hatch near the water's edge, freshwater crustaceans and small forage fish. Larger trout must sustain themselves by eating more small fish, yabbies, and even juveniles of their own kind!

Catching Trout

One of the trout's greatest attributes is its wide acceptance of all manner of fishing techniques. They are caught bait fishing, lure fishing, trolling and fly fishing.

Bait fishing is probably the most popular method for catching trout and can be conducted from the shore or a boat using a light casting tackle.

Most anglers opt for a weighted bait to assist them in casting. However, far more fish will be caught by suspending a worm or mudeye below a light bubble or quil float.

One method that reaps great results in

'Bait fishing is probably the most popular method for catching trout.'

BELOW: A beautifully marked 'wild' brown trout from Lake Dartmouth, northern Victoria.

lakes and dams, involves slow trolling a mudeye or worm behind a set of flasher blades, known commonly as 'cowbells'. In some impoundments, good hauls of native fish, particularly Macquarie perch, are also encountered using this technique.

In rivers and streams, best bait fishing results will be obtained using the bubble float rig, although many anglers concede that lure fishing covers more territory, and is a better producer of trout than bait.

Among the popular lure patterns are the spinning blade designs, various spoons, small diving plugs and miniature bucktail jigs.

Lake anglers also have a good deal of success using lures on trout. For shore stompers, casting is of prime importance and the heavier bladed spinners, the Australian made Baltic Minnow, spoons and the Cobra-style winged casting lures are all common fish takers.

Boat-based anglers usually slow troll for trout using the famed Helin Flatfish or its many imitators, diving plugs and wet flies. Cowbells are often set ahead of the lure as an added attractor, and in summer, weighted lead lines are sometimes employed to take the lure down to the thermoclines.

FRESHWATER TROLLING
Fishing on the Move

A wide range of freshwater species — both natives and 'exotic' imports — can be captured by trolling lures, flies or natural baits behind a boat. Here's how . . .

Trolling is trailing a lure, fly or bait at the end of a line, from a moving vessel. Although sometimes decried as the 'lazy angler's' fishing method, trolling requires skill and knowledge to be productive and satisfying.

Some ardent trollers argue that this method is, in its own way, as much of an art as fly fishing. Art or not, there is no more effective way to fish at varying depths over wide expanses of lakes and reservoirs and in the long reaches of navigable rivers.

Trolling — never to be confused with trawling — enables the angler to cover more fishable areas more quickly than any other sportfishing method.

Australian articles on freshwater trolling have tended to concentrate on trout, but trolling is also highly successful with many of our native sportfish. Some large lakes in New South Wales and Victoria contain mixed populations of exotic and indigenous species. In these fisheries it is common for a troller trying for trout to catch Murray cod and golden perch as well, especially if using a lure resembling a yabby.

Selecting a Boat

The boat for trolling can be powered by motor, man or wind. On some waterways, such as Lake Burley Griffin in the heart of Canberra, even rented, pedal-powered paddleboats are sometimes used to great effect!

Of course, motor boats are most commonly used, as sailboats are not sufficiently manoeuvrable. Rowboats can help impart a fish-attracting action to the lure, but demand too much energy for long sessions. Canoes require less energy and are ideal in tight spots, rivers and quiet waters, but they cannot be used on large, exposed waterways without risk to the occupants.

The choice of a motorised trolling boat will depend largely on the type of area most commonly fished. As trolling is the best angling method for large lakes and reservoirs, a boat which can be safely operated in almost any weather on such waters is an obvious choice.

Perhaps the best all-round boat is a stable aluminium or fibreglass runabout up to about five metres long, the minimum size being about four metres. It should ideally have a transom well, comfortable seating, a canopy, two swivelling seats up front and forward steering.

Outboard motors are the most suitable power units for freshwater trolling boats. Appropriate horsepower depends on a number of variables including the weight of the boat, the number of people usually carried

and the average distance to be travelled. An ideal rig is one which will plane with three adults on board, yet troll smoothly and slowly enough at idling speed.

With fibreglass and aluminium boats from four to five metres long, experience has shown that 25 horsepower is the maximum outboard motor size which will allow sufficiently slow trolling speeds.

A 25 horsepower motor will also drive a well-loaded runabout of up to 4.5 metres at planing speeds, ensuring fast travelling to the area to be trolled.

A motor which is to be used for both driving and trolling must be well-tuned for constant smooth idling. Should trolling speed still be a little too fast, a low-pitch propeller can be fitted, a sea-anchor drogue used, or a bucket can be dragged behind the boat.

Another option, though one not often used by Australian anglers, is 'back trolling' or reversing the boat. This enables many boats to troll more slowly than conventional forward trolling.

Lure Selection

Select lures which closely resemble, especially in action and colour, the natural food of the fish sought: yabbies for trout and most native species in many parts of New South Wales, southern Queensland and Victoria; forage fish or whitebait in Tasmania and small mullet in northern Australia.

Flatfish in frog and perch scale colours or patterns most closely resemble the yabby, which can vary in colour from very dark green or black with touches of light green, to very dark green or black with touches of orange.

The Tasmanian Devil lure in combinations of these colours has been remarkably successful in Australia's freshwater impoundments in recent years.

These lures are consistent fish-takers in impoundments such as Lakes Eucumbene,

PREVIOUS PAGE: Dawn over Lake Toolondo, western Victoria, as an angler prepares for a day's trout trolling. Much of the best inland trolling action comes during the change of light periods at dawn and dusk.
TOP: Success on Dartmouth Dam in the form of a good brown. Note the number and spread of outfits — legal in Victoria, but not on NSW trout waters, where only one outfit per angler is permitted.
ABOVE: An Atlantic salmon trolled up from a canoe on Jindabyne.
OPPOSITE: A chinook or quinnat taken on a trolled minnow lure.

Jindabyne and Tantangara in the Snowy Mountains and Dartmouth Dam in Victoria.

In Burrinjuck Reservoir, a mixed-species fishery, anglers commonly take rainbow trout, brown trout and small Murray cod or golden perch on one of these lures in the same trolling session.

In the north, the Nilsmaster Invincible is fatal to various species including barramundi.

In Tasmania, Devon and Tasmanian Devil lures snare many good trout.

Lure Size

Lures come in various sizes. A general rule is the bigger the fish you are after, the bigger the lure. For average-to-large trout, the most popular Flatfish sizes are F7 and X4. Both will take good Murray cod too, and some anglers replace the manufacturer's hooks with heavier ones when trolling for extra-large fish.

Celta and Mepps spinners are also popular with trollers. These seem to provide fewer hook-ups from strikes than the Flatfish-type, and have the advantage of being comparable with bait, such as worms. Any bait or piece of weed caught on the treble hooks of a Flatfish-type lure renders it useless. However, the attractiveness of a Celta or Mepps spinner is enhanced and its action unimpeded by the addition to its treble hook of one or several succulent worms.

Trolling with Flies

Most freshwater trollers use metal, plastic or wooden lures, but quite a few prefer flies, particularly for trout.

Tied on No 4 or No 6 hooks, wet flies such as the Red and Black Matuka, Green Matuka, Bucktail, Mrs Simpson, Muddler Minnow, Craig's Night-time, Green Whitebait and Taihape Tickler are commonly used, sometimes in conjunction with a dropper — another, usually smaller, fly hanging off the main line on a piece of heavier line about 10 cm long. The dropper is fixed about 20 cm in front of the terminal fly and the rig in action creates the illusion of a large fish or aquatic insect chasing a smaller one.

Fly trolling is most effective when fish are feeding on the surface. An unweighted fly, trolled very slowly, say, 80 metres behind the

ABOVE: Netting a keeper brown. Note the hessian sack hanging from the gunwale into the water for keeping the catch fresh on a warm inland day.
INSET ABOVE RIGHT: One of the deadliest of all Aussie trout trolling techniques is the use of a live or fresh-dead mudeye (dragonfly larvae) rigged behind cowbell-style flashers or attractors.
LEFT: This pretty rainbow took a Matuka fly trolled deep with leadcore line.

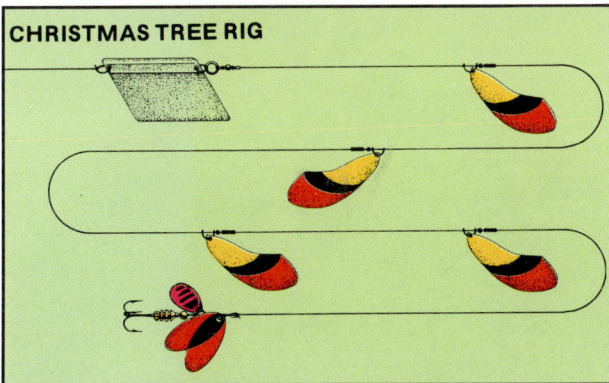

CHRISTMAS TREE RIG

The Christmas Tree or Cowbell rig consists of a series of metal blades rotating freely on a length of light wire. A keel or stabiliser is usually placed at the top of the rig to reduce line twist.

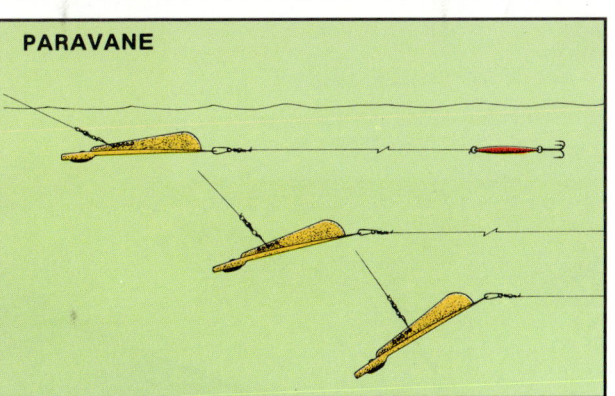

PARAVANE

Paravanes use water pressure to pull the line and lure down into the depths. They are made from plastic, metal or a combination of those materials. Many paravanes are adjustable for depth.

boat and on, or just a few centimetres below the surface, will take rising fish when all other lures fail.

Flies will also attract fish in deeper water. A fly is, after all, only a lure made from fur and feathers.

To fish flies deep, lead core line can be used. More simply, split shot or similar weights can be attached about a metre ahead of the terminal fly or the dropper. Obviously, a good length of line has to be let out to allow the flies to sink and run deep.

A heavy spoon, spinner or plug-type lure can also be used with a fly dropper and, depending on the weight of the main lure, may not need lead.

Fish Attractors

In major trout lakes, trollers have found that fish attractors, otherwise known as 'Bolos', 'Ford Fenders', 'Christmas Trees', 'Cow Bells' or 'Gang Spinners', not only increase catches, but help keep the lure down without lead.

The fish attractors — hookless blades revolving around a length of wire — are more conspicuous to fish than a single lure, but they have the disadvantage of creating great tension on the line and depriving the angler of some of the 'feel' of hooked fighting fish.

More false strikes occur with fish attractors than with a single lure, as fish sometimes attack the blades rather than the lure. However, fish attractors will generally produce more fish, especially in lakes and reservoirs where fish numbers have declined so that they have to be drawn to the lure from a wide area. In this case, a single trolled lure could go unnoticed.

BELOW: Six fine rainbow trout trolled from a canoe on Lake Jindabyne.
BOTTOM: Browns are also responsive to the stealthy approach of a canoe. This one took a flatfish.

Fish attractors may also be teamed with bait and flies. A hook baited with worms, wood grubs or mudeyes and tied behind fish attractors can be devastating, prompting more strikes than a lure.

Paravanes

For trollers who do not want the added weight and bulk of sinkers and fish attractors, or the expense of lead core line, but nevertheless want to get that lure down deep, a paravane is the answer.

A paravane is simply a hydrofoil which, like a bib on a deep-diving lure, is designed to cut or plane downwards when pulled through the water.

In contrast to a bib on a lure, however, the paravane is attached to the lure by about a metre of line (that is, a leader), and will tow the lure to the depths. Bibbed or deep-diving lures can still be used with the paravane, but the latter will outweigh the effect of the smaller bib on a deep-diving lure.

TOP: A hire boat on Tasmania's famous Lake Pedder. Unfortunately this one-time trophy lake now produces very few fish over 3 or 4 kg.

ABOVE: Freshwater trolling isn't only about trout! These two golden perch or yellowbelly were taken from the Namoi River in north-western NSW.

'Some sturdy but lightweight plastic paravanes are on the market, and these are suited to freshwater trolling.'

TROLLING SPEED CRITICAL

The critical factor in trolling, likely to make the difference between productive and non-productive fishing, is trolling speed.

Boat speed influences the action of the lure and affects its depth. Some lures will only work at a very slow trolling speed; the higher the speed, the closer the terminal gear will be to the surface. Too much speed is the most common mistake in freshwater trolling.

Trolling speed, particularly when using plug-type lures such as the Flatfish, should be no faster than a slow walking pace; about half a metre per second.

When trolling for northern species such as barramundi, and when using some spoon-type lures or others such as the Baltic Minnow and Wonder Wobbler, the speed may be slightly faster.

Trollers should follow the manufacturer's instructions for rigging the various types of paravanes and should troll only one paravane per boat. Anglers who feel sufficiently confident to use two paravanes should rig them only to rods mounted on opposite sides of the boat.

There are some sturdy, but lightweight plastic paravanes on the market, which are suited to freshwater trolling.

Terminal Rigs

Just as there are various lures and flies for different fish species, there are various terminal rigs for different trolling depths and environments.

The line-to-lure rig, when used with a bibbed or diving lure, will run far enough below the surface to take species such as barramundi. However, many of the species found in northern freshwater have strong, sharp teeth, calling for a wire or heavy monofilament leader up to 30 cm long between line and lure.

The straight line-to-fly and the dropper and fly combination, both need a weight or sinker except when surface trolling.

Fish attractors make terminal rigs a little more complex. A main line — that is, the line above the fish attractors — of about 4 kg or more, is needed to withstand the drag of the attractors. When trolling for average-sized trout and native species such as golden perch and silver perch, a trace or leader of lighter line, say 3 to 4 kg. is tied between attractors and lure, fly or bait hook. This gives the fish a sporting chance and also increases the odds of recovering the expensive attractors when only the lure is snagged. The theory is that the lighter trace between lure and attractor breaks before the main line rigged above the attractor.

Fish attractors impair the action of most plug-type lures when the latter are tied too near the attractors, so a leader of at least 1 to 1.5 metres is needed. Flies and bait hooks

should be tied about half a metre away from the attractors.

Swivels are vital in any trolling rig. A keel is also important with fish attractors. On straight line-to-lure rigs, a medium-sized snap swivel of appropriate strength should be tied between lure and line.

With fish attractors, use swivels between the main line and the keel at the head of the attractors; between the keel and the front end of the attractor wire; between the rear end of the attractor wire and the trace; and between the end of the trace and the lure.

This last swivel should be of the snap type, to allow quick change of lures.

Keels used at the head of fish attractors should be the large plastic type, although to achieve greater depth, some trollers use lead keels. Despite swivels, plastic keels still have a tendency to flip around or spin, imparting a slow twist to the main line. A small piece of lead pinched into a hole drilled near the outer edge of the keel will prevent this.

Rod and Reel

A few north Australian and western New South Wales anglers still troll with heavy handlines. This arguably requires less skill than fishing with rods, and does not offer as much sport.

In New South Wales, in proclaimed trout waters where other species may be present, only one rod to each angler may be used. This raised the question: what type of rod and reel should be used for trolling?

The perfectionists and well-heeled anglers insist on custom-built graphite rods with the finest reels available; but average anglers generally settle for a balanced rig which can be used both for spin-fishing on a stream and for trolling.

Good, versatile spinning rod and reel outfits can be bought for about $60 to $80. An example is a medium-strength, two-piece hollow or solid fibreglass rod, about two metres long, fitted with something better than simple wire guides.

This price should also cover the cost of a light spinning reel with metal-skirted spool capable of holding about 100 metres of 7 kg test line with ball-bearing races, ambidextrous handle, a retrieve ratio between 3.8:1 and 4.5:1 and especially a smooth, readily-adjustable drag system.

The angler wanting a bit more may prefer a light-to-medium baitcasting reel and rod, but whatever the choice, both rod and reel must be relatively light.

Successful Trolling

The real key to successful trolling is a knowledge of the behavioural patterns and preferred habitat of the target species.

For instance, Murray cod prefer relatively warm water and, as with golden perch and mangrove jack, generally seek out snags or fallen timber for cover. So, logical places to troll for them are around such obstructions.

Locating Trout

Trout prefer cooler water, from 10 to 18°C. They are found in summer in our larger southern lakes and reservoirs in the 'thermocline'; a level between the warmer surface water and the cooler bottom water.

The thermocline occurs at varying depths, according to location and time of year, and the troller who can locate it with a thermometer on a line, depth sounder or through experience, and then get his terminal gear down to the appropriate operating depth, will catch more trout than the one who goes in blind and sinks his gear to only two or three metres when the thermocline is, say, eight or 10 metres down.

Most trollers, especially those hunting large, lake-dwelling trout, usually fish too shallow, content to let their lures work at depths of one to five metres. Occasionally, a fish will rise from deeper water to accept the challenge, but it is far more profitable to get the lure down among the fish, which may be at a depth of six to 20 metres.

Trollers chasing trout should also know that brown trout are often loners, and take up individual territories, while rainbow trout are more gregarious, often roaming in small schools. From these details, the troller will be able to generalise that, if one or two rainbows are taken in the same spot, a patch of them has probably been found and so troll over that spot several times in succession.

A muddy bank or shoreline marked with yabby holes is obviously worth close trolling, especially with a lure resembling a yabby.

Trolling near, or over the tops of submerged trees, is also worthwhile, as fish will congregate where good combinations of food and cover occur.

Many shoreline characteristics and landforms give the angler clues to the most likely location of fish. Lines of large rocks and boulders running into the water point to underwater rocky cover, and tree-studded ridges, which extend into a lake, especially a man-made one, will usually indicate dead trees and other material jutting from the lake bed.

Depth Sounders

Commonsense methods of locating fish can be reinforced with a depth sounder. Simple flasher-type sounders are relatively inexpensive, do not require any complex installation process, are extremely sensitive and more than adequate for freshwater application.

With only a little experience, the troller using such a sounder is able to determine instantly the depth of the water being fished and the type of bottom — muddy, rocky or weedy — as well as the presence and depth of submerged obstructions.

Equally important is the ability to perceive

ABOVE: Downriggers are gaining popularity in Australia, especialy among freshwater anglers trolling for trout in large impoundments. BELOW: A fence line disappearing into a lake backwater. Such a piece of structure could easily produce fish in an otherwise relatively featureless expanse of water.

ABOVE: A haul of brown trout and one lone redfin perch taken on the troll.

'The thermocline occurs at varying depths according to location and time of year.'

RIGHT: This budding junior angler looks justifiably proud of his first two freshwater fish — a fine Macquarie perch and a brown trout. A brace of fish like this could easily start such a youngster on the road to bigger things.
FAR RIGHT: High-tech trolling; baitcasters, depth sounders and downriggers.

A FEW HINTS

When retrieving line use the 'pump' method: lift the rod tip; pull back on the rod; then, dropping the rod forward again, wind down on the slack line which has been created by the initial back pull. Simply repeat the process until the lure is in the boat. The pump retrieve will impart a stop-go action to the lure and increase the chances of a strike during the retrieve. Moreover, the pump action will help prevent the line being wound too tightly around the spool.

People who smoke while fishing should be careful about handling lures, flies and particularly bait. Carefully controlled experiments using smokers and non-smokers in lure trolling have proved that, other things being equal, the non-smoker, or the smoker who takes care not to taint the lure with the taste or smell of nicotine, will catch more fish.

When smoking, do not handle the terminal gear; let a non-smoker do it for you or carry a towel and wipe your hands thoroughly before touching the gear. In fact, the smell and taste of a lure can be enhanced, particularly when trout fishing, by rubbing slime from your first catch on to all lures being trolled. Experiments have shown that this can improve the strike rate.

Here is a final word of advice that applies to all other fishing as much as to trolling. Before venturing out to fish an unfamiliar waterway, seek information from local anglers. If you share their interest and their enthusiasm for sportfishing, they may even take you trolling.

the presence of fish and the depths at which they are holding. Very experienced users can even tell the approximate size of the fish by the size and intensity of the 'blip' or 'flash' on the scanner dial.

Paying Out Line

Allow line to run out by loosening the brake rather than throwing the bail arm over or disengaging the gears. The latter method can cause tangles near the reel and jerk the outgoing terminal rig so badly that treble hooks become caught up with each other, or with the leader or main line.

Experienced trollers loosen their reel brakes and lower the terminal gear into the water, making sure that the treble hooks are not snagged and the lure is working correctly. Then, they smoothly let out enough line to ensure the gear will not break the surface once it has begun to sink, and then increase the speed of the boat to about eight knots, letting line off the reel as they go. This method, known as a 'speed run', substantially reduces the time taken to let out line.

Of course, once sufficient line has been let out during the speed run, the boat is immediately slowed to the normal trolling speed. This speed-run method of laying out line can be used only when the two or three trollers act in unison; confusion reigns if one or two already have line fully out.

With sufficient line out, the reel brake should be tightened so that there will be no line loss until a heavy and continuous drag is felt on the line. The weight of line and gear should not cause the brake to release more line. Conversely, a hard, sustained run from a

big fish after the strike and hook-up, or the drag caused by a firmly snagged lure, must force a well-adjusted brake system to release line smoothly as the weight of the drag demands. A common mistake in trolling is to have the brake set too lightly.

Rod Holders

Use of rod holders makes trolling more relaxing between strikes, providing the holders are of good quality and correctly set.

A rod holder must be designed to allow the angler to pick up the rod quickly once a strike or hook-up has occurred.

Holders at the sides of a boat must keep the rods at 90 degrees to the centre line of the boat and at an angle of about 15 degrees to the water surface. The rod holder at the stern, with three trollers, must keep the rod vertical and the line, clear of boat and motor, over the centre of the stern.

Adjusting Speed

Lack of strikes or hook-ups on the first few trolling runs, means the depth and speed of

ABOVE: Murray cod regularly snaffle slow-trolled lures, particularly deep-running plugs. For best results, lures need to be dragged close to cover, such as submerged timber and rock bars.

BELOW: The way of the future — this Victorian angler is trolling Lake Dartmouth with the full array of sophisticated tackle and downriggers. This use of such technology can undoubtedly improve results in certain situations.

the lures should be altered. With two or three lines trolling, the depth of at least one lure should be changed. To adjust depth, release or retrieve line.

The speed of the lures can be changed just as easily. Steering the boat in a long, slow, 'S' pattern will speed the port lure and slow the starboard lure as a gradual turn to starboard is made. The converse effect will be achieved with a turn to port. The 'S' pattern should be tried before changing the boat's speed.

If flies or natural baits are being trolled, a good practice is to hold the rod and jerk the tip up and down every 30 seconds or so to move the terminal gear.

Several warnings apply for the helmsmen: no tight turns; no cutting across points of land; no steering the boat sharply through snags when a lot of line is out.

If 90 metres of line is out, the radius of the turning circle should be no less than 180 metres, and when on a trolling run, always keep in mind the distance between boat and lure, remembering that the lure will never respond quickly to a sharp change in boat direction.

At trolling speed, with 90 metres of line out, the lure will take some three minutes to reach the point where the boat first changed direction! By then, the effect on the lure of the new direction of troll will be much diminished, particularly if the original change of direction of the boat was not pronounced.

Ready for Action

With preparations over, the tackle ready and the boat in the chosen trolling area, it is time to let out the lines, and select the line of troll or direction of the trolling run, allowing for any wind drift during the run and, if possible, positioning the boat so that you will be trolling with the wind. This makes the boat easier to steer than if it is headed into the wind.

Moreover, if the fish, especially trout, are on or anywhere near the surface on a breezy, they will be facing upwind, towards the oncoming lure.

Ideally, have no more than two trollers in a boat. However. three are possible; one on each side of the boat and the third over the centre of the stern. To prevent tangles and foul-ups, the centre line should be weighted more heavily and kept shorter than the lines trolled from the rods at the sides of the boat.

Do not cast any troll lure or terminal rig back into the wake. Many things can go wrong when the rig is in the air or as it hits the water, and many hours' trolling can be wasted before the angler realises the lure has been caught-up or fouled and has not been working. This is a frequent problem when multiple treble-hook lures such as Flatfish are cast at the start of a run.

Once the boat has slowed to trolling speed, the terminal gear should be placed smoothly in the water, the reel brake loosened and enough line let out gradually to allow the gear to sink. Always maintain a light finger-touch on the revolving spool to prevent backlash.

Tip Action

Most lures and rigs will set up a certain rhythmic action on the rod tip. Experience teaches anglers the actions which different lures and rigs impart to a rod tip.

Learn to detect immediately when tip action departs from normal, because this usually means something is wrong with the lure. A gentle bump from a fish which is not hooked, can wrap treble hooks around leader line. Weed through which the lure may have passed can affect lure action adversely. Even grass stalks and twigs can catch on the line, as it cuts through the water surface, and run down the line to the lure, preventing it from working correctly. In such instances, a change

LANDING FISH

Gaffs are rarely used in freshwater fishing outside of barramundi waters. Use a net to boat fish.

The correct size of the net mouth varies with the size of the species, but a general-purpose landing net will have a mouth at least 65 cm in diameter and an extendable handle which can be folded for out-of-the-way storage.

The net mesh must be very heavy nylon monofilament or thick, two-ply or three-ply, tightly woven nylon. Cotton net mesh of thin, limp thread, will too easily snag hooks and lead to frustrating tangles.

It is sometimes not easy to use a landing net without knocking the fish off the lure or getting line caught on or around the net. For safe, effective netting, the fish should be played out until it is lying quietly on the surface. The netsman should first wet the mesh to make sure the net will form its normal cone-shape in the water; then bring its mouth up to the fish's head and in one smooth movement, quickly slide the net right over the fish, before bringing the mouth upwards and lifting both net and fish from the water. The net should not be lifted until the whole fish is in.

If the fish darts out before it can be fully enclosed by the net, it should be settled down again and the netting operation repeated. Indiscriminate jabs and swings at the fish to try to get it in the net are unwise, leading to lost fish and strained relations between angler and netsman!

ABOVE: These anglers have taken a break from trolling to pull ashore for some lunch. The middle part of the day is often less productive than the early morning and late afternoon…
TOP RIGHT:…however, rules were made to be broken! This lovely brown trout fell to a lure trolled behind a canoe in the middle of a bright sunny day.
RIGHT: Believe it or not, this is fresh water! The scene is Lake Jindabyne in a 120 kph-plus gale during June. Storms such as these can hit at any time and with little warning on our high-country lakes. Obviously, they pose an extreme hazard to small boat operators.

in rod-tip action may be the only way to detect a lure problem.

It is important to be able to detect the difference between a strike and a snag; sometimes they appear very similar. A strike will usually cause the rod tip to buck violently first and then, if the fish is hooked, to bend into that characteristic fighting curve. A snag will bend the rod more slowly into that curve, but there will be no initial jerk or strike action. Instead, the rod will start to bend as the lure is held on the snag and will continue to bend smoothly until the reel brake begins to operate.

If more than one person is trolling, all other lines should be wound in and the snagged line retrieved as the boat is reversed toward the snag.

At no time should the snagged line be allowed to go slack; nor should excessive pressure be put on the line until the boat has reversed over the snag, allowing the lure to be pulled in the direction opposite to that in which it was trolled. Only then should the rod tip be worked up and down and from side to side to help free the lure hooks from the snag.

Line Tension

Once a fish has struck, some trollers grab their rods from the holders and pull back hard on the rod to set the hook. In freshwater trolling

'Cotton net mesh of thin, limp thread will too easily snag hooks and lead to frustrating tangles.'

this is usually unnecessary; if the hooks are sharp and the reel brake tensioned correctly, and if the rod was in a holder at the time of strike, the hook should be soundly set.

If a fish is definitely hooked, the motor should be stopped or at least put in neutral. All other trolling lines should be retrieved quickly and kept away from the line being played.

Once the other lines are in, rods and gear should be placed well out of the way and only the trace man or netsman should be near the angler.

Because a fish can use the weight of a lure and terminal gear to help shake the hook from its mouth, the line should be kept taut throughout the fight, particularly if the fish jumps or struggles on the surface.

Wind drift must be allowed for in keeping the correct tension on the line. If the wind is in the angler's face, the boat will be drifting away from the fish and he will have to wind in a little more slowly so as not to skull-drag the fish and pull the hook out. If the wind is behind him, the boat will be drifting towards the fish and to avoid slack, line may have to be retrieved more quickly.

You should try to play the fish from the upwind side, as the drift will help keep the line taut and prevent the fish from running under the boat or around the motor.

Keeping the Catch Alive

Fish can be kept alive in the boat until the end of the trolling session, in a live bait tank or in a keeper net hung over the side.

Alternatively, the fish can be wrapped in a wet hessian bag and stowed in a shady spot on the bottom of the boat.

Another way is to put the bag, with fish inside and neck tied, over the side like a keeper net. Never use plastic bags, or sacks made from materials which do not 'breathe'.

TROUT TACTICS

Trolling for Deepwater Summer Trout

Robert Little/Auscape International

Trout are often at their most active during the hot summer months, particularly in our large dams. Paradoxically, they can be difficult to catch. One answer is to troll deep.

Trolling is one of the most popular methods of catching trout. It can be a simple, relaxed technique — run a lure out and cruise slowly round the lake. Sometimes the fish co-operate and you can take good catches.

However, there are times — particularly in the hot summer months — when the trout just aren't interested; or so it seems. After hours of fruitless trolling fishermen come in complaining the trout are 'off the bite'.

Of course it is usually just the opposite. Trout feed actively over summer, enjoying the abundance of food generally available at this time. So, if the trout are out hunting, why aren't they being hooked? Often the answer is simple: the fishermen's lures are working shallow while the trout are working deep. Trolling tactics that enable you to get a lure down there where the trout are feeding is what this article deals with.

Why They are Down There

Basically, trout swim deep in summer for two reasons: comfort and food.

Trout are cold-water fish. The surface waters of many of our dams become

ABOVE: A pair of small boat anglers trolling close to a steep shoreline in Lake Eucumbene, in south-western NSW. During the heat of summer, trout seek out deeper, cooler water, and anglers need to be versatile in order to reach these suspended fish.

uncomfortably warm for trout during the long, hot, sunny days of summer. Although they may still rise to the surface late and early in the day and at night to feed on insects, they will spend the day in the deeper, cooler water.

Secondly, there is a good deal of food to be found in deep water. For instance, weed beds can host big populations of yabbies, shrimp and insect larvae. While both of our main trout species — browns and rainbows — will take a wide range of food items from the lake bed right through the water column to the surface, browns in particular like grubbing for large prey on the bottom.

Trolling deep can definitely boost your summertime catches of brown and rainbow trout, as well as those other, rarer salmonids also available in some Australian waters; the Atlantic salmon, chinook (or quinnat) salmon and brook trout.

How Deep is Deep?

Okay, in summer on the trout lakes you should troll deep. But what does 'deep' mean? Generally that can be interpreted as more than three or four metres under the surface and sometimes you might even troll a lure or bait down 20 metres or more.

Few of the small lures commonly trolled for trout will dive, unaided, deeper than two or three metres. Trout swimming at five to 10 metres might no see those lures and, even if they do, might not bother rising to investigate. You need something to take your lure down to where the trout are.

How to Get Down There

There are several ways of getting lures down deep. Some are simple, some sophisticated, and some require special tackle while others demand nothing more than cheap items found in most laundries. These techniques involve downriggers, wire lines and leadcore lines.

A 'downrigger' takes your lure to a known depth. At their most sophisticated they are expensive commercial units featuring aerodynamic 'bombs', wire line, metal spools, winding handle (or even automatic retrieve facility) and depth indicator.

The trolling line is clipped onto the bomb and lowered to the required depth. With a wind of the handle the bomb, and therefore running depth of the lure, can be raised or lowered easily. When a trout strikes, the line is pulled from the clip on the bomb and you fight the fish in the usual way.

Cowbells and Ford-Fenders

In normal, straightline, close-to-the-surface trolling many experienced anglers use what are commonly called Cowbells or Ford-Fenders. These are small blades that spin and flash when pulled through the water. They seem to arouse a trout's curiosity and, when investigating these strange flashes, the fish is likely to spot the bite-sized bait or lure trailing half-a-metre or so behind.

However, when used on the fishing line, they take a lot of the fight out of hooked fish. The trout has to drag all the hardware through the water as it struggles on the end of the line. For that reason some anglers treat Cowbells and Fenders with disdain, though they definitely can increase catches.

In deep trolling, these flashy attractors can be used on the downrigger, tied on behind the bomb sinker. A small peg or commercial line release clip is then tied onto the chain of attractors. Now, when a trout strikes, the line pops free — the heavy attractors stay with the downrigger line and the fish can be fought cleanly.

All this takes time and practice to perfect, and some terrible tangles might be experienced along the way, but with a little perseverence it is a high efficiency, low-cost trolling technique.

'It does take some of the fight out of the trout, and for that reason is rejected, like most heavy attractors, by some anglers.'

Wired for Depth

Now, for the next technique — wire lining. A wire line is just that, a line of wire rather than the usual monofilament nylon. The whole line is not wire, but rather a section of around 20 to 40 metres joined with swivels to the main line and a trace. This thin but heavy (compared with nylon) wire line runs deep once a weight is added.

Uncoated trace wire is suitable for this method. Use wire with a breaking strength of about 8 kg. On the trace, and immediately behind the wire section, tie, using swivels, a trolling sinker. This is shaped more or less like a fat-bellied, front-heavy aeroplane with stubby wings angled down. Pulled through the water, this sinker takes the line down through a combination of its own weight and the water pressure on the 'wings' or vanes. The nylon trace behind this sinker is one to two metres long.

The sinker can be replaced with a para-vane. Provided steady strain is applied by towing the paravane, then water pressure on its flat top surface keeps it angling down. A trout grabbing the lure tied to a trace from the back of the paravane 'trips' the paravane and it lies parallel to the main line and trace, providing little interference to the retrieval of the fish. However, it does take some of the fight out of the trout, and for that reason is rejected, like most heavy attractors, by some anglers.

Anglers who use this method regularly will often buy a bakelite centrepin reel and a rod with metal or strong metal-oxide runners — the wire section in the line will damage most standard reels and cheap ceramic runners with regular use.

Lead-core Lines

Like the wire line, a lead-core line is just what the name suggests. It has a core of thin lead wire. The result is a line that looks something like a fly-casting line but is heavier. This extra weight takes the lure down deeper.

A lead core line does not run as deep as a wire line or a line on a downrigger. However, it will troll as deep as 4 or 5 metres. Lead core lines are usually colour-coded so that you can see how much line is off the spool. With experience, you will be able to estimate the likely depth your lure is running with any combination of boat speed and line length.

Optimum Boat Speed

Boat speed affects trolling depth because the faster the boat is moving, the greater the 'drag' on the line pushing it towards the surface. Trolling speeds for trout are usually slower than walking pace, that is around two to three knots.

As with the wire line, the lead-core line is tied onto the main line and a trace of about two metres. (No swivels this time but a knot

OPPOSITE TOP: A fine haul of big rainbow trout, Atlantic salmon and a lone brown; all taken while deep trolling with lead-core line in Lake Jindabyne, NSW.

TOP LEFT: Even in summer those alpine mornings can be brisk! Here the editor slow trolls a fly on lead-core line. Note that all the lead-core has been paid-out, revealing the dacron backing on his small baitcaster.

ABOVE: The end result of some wire-line deep trolling on a stormy summer's evening; almost 3 kg of fighting-fit Jindabyne rainbow.

D•I•Y

Commercial downriggers are usually rather expensive and a fully funtional, cost-saving trolling downrigger can be made with very little effort at home. All that's required is a handline, large sinker and a clothes peg. In this case the clothes peg is slipped onto the handline, then the sinker tied to the end of the line. Make certain you run the line through the hole behind the jaws of the peg, rather than gripped by the jaws. Lower the sinker to the desired depth, run the lure back about 10 metres, and await a strike.

A large 450 gram snapper sinker makes a good bomb in this case. Putting a vane on the sinker will stop the handline spinning and tangling. Another way is to drill a hole through the sinker so that it runs like a torpedo through the water. One or two small, ball-bearing swivels tied into the handline are extra insurance against line twist.

instead; the best is the nail knot, relatively easy to tie after a little practice.)

With these techniques either lures or baits can be trolled. These include small wobblers like diving minnows, the Flatfish and the Baltic Minnow. Freshwater wet flies such as the matukas, Mrs Simpsons and other streamer patterns can also be used to good effect, especially when trolled on lead-core lines. In inlaid impoundements, baits such as worms, mudeyes and small minnows are often trolled for trout.

Local Knowledge Invaluable

There is nothing like local knowledge and frequent trips to the same dam to provide a picture of how its trout population is likely to behave in different conditions.

For instance Great Lake, in the central highlands of Tasmania, is comparatively cool and comfortable for trout year-round. But in water about six to 10 metres deep (and 100 to 200 metres from shore) there are several large weedbeds, the favourite feeding place for big brown trout.

Anglers trolling shallower water closer to shore are catching small browns, forced off the weed beds by aggressive fish in their prime, and they are catching rainbow trout too. But knowledgeable anglers working the deep weedbeds are consistently taking bigger catches of better-conditioned browns.

In central-southern New South Wales, the surface waters of dams like Burrinjuck and Wyangala become warm during summer, sending trout down below the 'thermocline' for most of the day. The thermocline is the distinct border between the warmer surface water and the colder water beneath.

To catch fish here consistently during the day means trolling a lure or bait in the cooler water under the thermocline. In the deep main section of Burrinjuck Dam, rainbow trout are caught at depths of at least 20 metres.

OPPOSITE TOP LEFT: This Eucumbene brown took a Flatfish lure trolled with the aid of a Canadian-made 'Scotty' downrigger.
OPPOSITE: A brown hooked on a fly behind lead-core blasts off just a few metres from the rod tip.
TOP: Spinning blade lures can also be employed successfully on deep-trolled gear, as evidenced by this fine rainbow.
ABOVE: Waiting for a strike on a hazy summer's day.

LURE FISHING FOR FRESHWATER NATIVES

Hard Challenges, Top Rewards

For a continent with a dearth of fresh water, Australia really hasn't done too badly when it comes to freshwater lure fishing. True, much of the limited fresh water we do have has been degraded, but despite this, for most Australians there is a freshwater lure-fishing spot within reach, even if it means a day's drive.

In many cases, finding freshwater lure fishing spots does take a little more effort. Being prepared to walk, or to use a canoe or small boat is almost essential. However, once the effort has been made, some water located and a few fish caught; those who make the effort and like it, often find themselves hooked!

Freshwater lure fishing for native Australian fish is not for those who are obsessed with catching large numbers of fish. It is for those who can appreciate the special magic of what has been called 'sweetwater'. It is for those who consider the challenge of working out a lure presentation, executing it and then feeling the crunching thud of a strike, both exciting and satisfying.

There is becoming less and less fresh water left in Australia that is capable of supporting native fish. The little we do have, along with the fish that reside there, should literally be treated as national treasures.

RIGHT: A beautiful Murray cod of almost 20 kg taken on a single-handed plugcasting outfit and Cotton Cordell Rattlin' Spot lure. Location was southern outback Queensland.

'Murray cod too, tend to hang around cover and larger specimens are quite happy in the murk of the inland rivers.'

BELOW: A canoe or similar lightweight vessel provides perfect access to those snag-filled backwaters where lure-eating natives live.
INSET: The payoff for some quiet paddling and accurate lure placement in this type of water could take the form of a solid golden perch or yellowbelly like this one.

Fishing for Australian Natives

Freshwater lure fishing can have an enjoyably unique Australian flavour. Overseas 'imports' such as trout and salmon are great; largemouth and smallmouth bass may be fine in the Great Lakes, United States. However, none have quite the same effect as a 'beer keg' of an Aussie Murray cod taking a lure at your feet, the tangible atmosphere of a hot afternoon's bass fishing, or a saratoga shouldering a surface plug down among the lily stems of a tropical lagoon.

The whole point about lure fishing for freshwater natives is to try it. If you enjoy the finer points of fishing, you'll almost certainly like it.

The native fish of primary interest to lure fishers in Australia are silver and golden perch (yellowbelly), Murray cod and close relatives, Australian bass, forktail catfish, Pacific tarpon, barramundi, sooty grunter and saratoga.

They're a diverse lot, living as they do from the tropic north to the cooler south, yet fundamental techniques work across the board. Techniques aimed at Murray cod, golden perch or bass using deep running lures, will work every bit as well on barramundi. Surface-lure presentations that tempt a saratoga, will have the same effect at sundown on a mid-summer bass stream. Midwater fishing styles suitable for silver perch, will score on forktail catfish or tarpon. Experienced bass fishers can't miss on sooty grunter and vice versa.

An angler can learn how to present one type of lure for one type of freshwater native, and yet use the same methods on a totally different fish in a totally different location — the common denominator being the same 'situation'.

It is important to look at each of the native lure targets in relation to their habits. Later we'll look at lure presentations to suit.

Silver and Golden Perch

Silver perch are a schooling fish which dwell in open water. They have a small mouth and an aggressive, competitive nature. They prefer moving water, yet care little whether it is crystalline or turbid brown.

Yellowbelly, as golden perch are commonly called, are a typical snag-dwelling fish, prone to spending long periods simply laying up in cover and only moving out into open water to feed when in a most aggressive mood. Larger specimens tend to be somewhat singular by nature; only congregating during upstream spawning migrations when there's a 'fresh' on.

Like the other Murray/Darling fishes, muddy (or turbid) water presents no problems to them and many a first-time angler has wondered how the fish can find lures in such dirty water. Clearer water does provide better lure fishing.

ABOVE: Not all Murray cod are giants. This spectacularly marked juvenile is about typical of those encountered today in most waters.
TOP RIGHT: Bass water near the Queensland/New South Wales border.
FAR RIGHT: Releasing the kind of bass that is no more than a memory in most areas these days. Two kilo-plus females like this are as rare as hen's teeth now.

Murray Cod

The blue-singleted, beer-gutted Ockers of Australian freshwater, Murray cod are singular, pugnacious and darned stroppy towards all and sundry when the mood takes them.

Murray cod too, tend to hang around cover and larger specimens are quite happy in the murk of the inland rivers. However, some of the best lure fishing to be had is for smaller specimens in clear, mountain headwater country.

Australian Bass

Living, as they do, along the heavily-populated eastern seaboard, bass are our most popular and most readily-available native lure target.

Bass follow the snag-dweller pattern, using timber, rock, weed and — in more urbanised water — car bodies or any other handy hang-outs.

Unlike golden perch and Murray cod, which only occasionally rise to the top to feed, bass feed extensively upon insects taken from the surface layer.

Forktail Catfish

Much maligned, and given such handles as 'turbid walloper', forktail catfish are long overdue for recognition as sporting lure takers.

Forktail catfish are an open-water fish caught just about anywhere. They don't fight all that vigorously, but are at least the equal of several others on a plate, and hit a lure as hard as any other fish.

Catfish are found throughout the north and as far south as the latitude of Newcastle.

Tarpon

Like the catfish, the tarpon is often overlooked when freshwater lure fishing is being discussed. This essentially estuarine fish habitually penetrates well into fresh water and ranges south past the Queensland/New South Wales border.

The tarpon is a schooling open-water fish, which may betray its presence by periodic air-gulping 'rises' to the surface.

They will feed anywhere from surface to bottom. Schools are aggressive, but hard to hook due to 'cast-iron' mouths.

'Bass feed extensively upon insects taken from the surface layer.'

ABOVE: Although many fish are released these days, there's nothing wrong with keeping an occasional specimen for the table.

Barramundi

Immature barra' spend the first years of their lives in fresh water, feeding and growing to sexual maturity before heading downstream to breed. A few larger barramundi are also found in fresh water.

Another classic snag dweller, the freshwater barra' can also be very moody, but the extent of that moodiness, may be a little exaggerated by anglers. When the mood takes them however, barramundi show the 'Mr Hyde-side' of their nature by doing such things as feeding with abandon in open water and creek mouths.

Sooty Grunter

Sooties, while tending to lay in cover waiting for a feed to come along, will move well away from cover in pursuit of food.

Competition is often the name of the game in heavily-populated tropical streams, with several sooties often vying for a lure at once.

If anything, sooty grunter are almost too aggressive; which makes them perhaps the easiest of all the freshwater natives to take on a lure.

Saratoga

Australia's very own living fossil, the beautiful and primitive saratoga, is purpose-built to feed from below.

High-mounted eyes and an upward-sloping mouth give away a saratoga's propensity towards taking surface lures.

'Competition is often the name of the game in heavily-populated tropical streams, with several sooties vying for a lure at once.'

Like the tarpon sometimes found in company with it, the solitary saratoga has an extremely hard mouth, making it very difficult to hook.

Saratoga have superb vision both above and below the water and have been observed tracking a cast lure before it lands.

Habits and Lure Choice

Once a basic understanding of the target fish's habits is at hand, a lure has to be chosen which matches. If fishing a snaggy stream likely to contain bass, Murray cod, golden perch or barramundi, a deep-running lure which was able to reach down among rocks and timber, would be a good choice.

'Low-dissolved oxygen levels and high water temperatures also make fish lethargic and casual about feeding.'

RIGHT: Tropical rainforest country of this type may produce jungle perch . . .
BELOW: . . . or the hard fighting sooty grunter.

A surface lure would be a bad choice except perhaps late in the afternoon or early in the morning, when bass or barra' are likely to be feeding from the surface.

Murray cod or golden perch are quite unlikely to take that surface lure at any time. Sooty grunter follow the pattern of surface feeding when the light dims as do saratoga. Saratoga may even take a surface lure in the middle of the day.

Tarpon, catfish and silver perch, being mid-water schooling fish, suit a presentation with a sinking lure which makes enough commotion to attract attention. Bladed spinners

'The very best anglers are constantly looking for cover that offers more.'

are ideal, they sink quickly, 'flutter' on the way down and the buzzing, flashing, blade is a real advertisement. Smaller bladed spinners also suit the silver perch's small mouth.

Factors Affecting Lure-Taking Mood

Fish don't have emotions. How they 'feel' is governed by their environment. We've referred to moods quite a bit so far, because that relates in human terms. But what actually happens to fish is that their behaviour is influenced by changes to their environment, such as light and dark, water temperature and the pH level of the water, or by biological factors such as baitfish migrations or breeding seasons. Many of these factors are also triggered by environmental changes such as

LEFT: A box full of freshwater hardware. There are thousands of dollars worth of lures here, but most anglers build up their collections over many, many years . . .
BELOW: . . . which is just as well, because country like this can be tough on lures!

seasonal warming of water, or the occurrence of a 'fresh'.

Most fish tend to feed more actively in dim light and this applies to freshwater lure fishing as much as any other type of fishing.

Water temperature is one of the most critical environmental influences. It's always important and sometimes vital to know what the water temperature is and how different temperatures affect the fish you're seeking.

Low water temperatures cause fish to develop 'lockjaw'. Snag dwellers snuggle back deep into cover and lie dormant. At such times it's difficult to get them to take a lure, unless one can literally be presented right on top of their noses. Presenting a lure deep into rock or timber, and then working it within striking distance of a 'doggo' barra', bass, golden perch or Murray cod, takes good water reading, combined with accurate casting of a lure right into the 'strike zone'.

High water temperatures affect the amount of dissolved oxygen water contains. Low-dissolved oxygen levels and high water temperatures also make fish lethargic and casual about feeding. They're simply not up and dashing about burning oxygen.

Gathering Data

Little data is available on the water temperature activity zones for Australian fish. A few anglers have worked out a fair idea for themselves — which they naturally tend to guard somewhat fiercely. The lack of published material really leaves the onus on the individual to observe, record and find out for themselves.

The acidity of alkalinity of water is a little easier to observe without instruments. As a general rule, pH is only affected to a degree which will have dramatic effect on fish behaviour by some noticeable phenomenon, such as an algae or weed-growth bloom that has died off, or a bushfire which has dumped large quantities of ash into the water.

Other more subtle alterations to pH do affect behaviour to an extent, but again, like the temperature influence, there's virtually no published literature.

Biological influences are more tangible. The times of year that barramundi feed actively before moving downstream to breed and then feed actively after breeding are well known — the former during the first rains of the wet, the latter as the rain eases.

The annual mullet run is another example of an observable phenomenon. Bass, feeding on juvenile mullet in northern New South Wales, aren't keen at all on surface lures for a few weeks there.

Reading Water

There is more to reading water than saying to yourself 'log here; cast lure'.

The very best anglers are constantly looking for cover that offers more. They're also constantly trying to work out what's good for fish, as opposed to what looks good from above the water.

Think about the criteria a fish would apply. What does a fish look for?

If there is current, all the snag inhabitors will look for cover providing a 'lie' where the current's force is broken — in effect a lee — behind rock, timber, a protruding point or an undercut bank.

The same fish also like a band of shade where they can lie in relative obscurity watching the world pass by. For example, the sooty grunter in a pacy north Queensland rainforest stream takes station in a spot where it can view the passing traffic. The angler should therefore pinpoint a spot where there's a lot of water movement.

In the middle of the day, sooties are reluctant to come too close to the surface, so a deeprunning lure is an obvious choice.

In the evening, when sooties are liable to rise to the surface and a breeze is plopping berries off overhanging trees, it may well pay to totally abandon snag fishing. Chances are that the fish will all be under the trees where feeding is easier and more profitable.

Impoundment Fishing

A lack of current brings a new scenario into being. What we're really talking about here is impoundment fishing, although the same situation does occur in long, still pools or isolated waterholes on a natural river. Without current, one fishy criteria can be dropped from water reading evaluation — the need for a current 'lee'.

The shade, shelter and passing 'traffic' factors still apply, but in dams there's a clear-cut critical difference between two classic 'points' — one of which has fish and one which hasn't.

Drowned timber in an impoundment tends to comprise standing trees. The vertical limbs of Australian hardwoods provide poor cover, as there is little shade. As well as that, fish lying in cover prefer to orient themselves horizontally, rather than stand on head or tail beside a vertical limb!

What does this have to do with fishing 'points'? Bays each side of a 'point' provide multiple routes for any fodder moving along the bank; but all must round a prominent point. One featuring trees with horizontal limbs, perhaps a big fallen tree, or particularly rock outcroppings rugged enough to provide cover is the place to look for golden perch and Murray cod in a dam. The same applies in one of those isolated muddy pools so characteristic of inland rivers. Ditto yet again for bass or forktail catfish in a large pool, and guess where lagoon barra' are likely to be found?

Reading Cover

By the time we've moved from a New South Wales impoundment to the lily lagoons of the tropical north, what is defined as cover can

lure tossers will go to any lengths to reach new water!
ABOVE: Others prefer the comforts of a canoe. Catch here is a fine golden perch.

'In the middle of the day, sooties are reluctant to come too close to the surface.'

ABOVE: Top End native fish water, where the prime targets are saratoga, barramundi, tarpon, sooty grunter, catfish and archers.

'The best way to fish a rock outcrop in a dam — which looks a likely holding place for golden perch and Murray cod — may not be to cast at all, but to troll.'

change. Instead of the tree snag discussed a moment ago, which nature has given horizontal limbs, 'cover' might be a weed bed or perhaps simply some lily pads.

Is the weed or the pads different to that gnarled old snag? Not really — although the snag probably has better fish-holding capability.

This is what's called 'prime' cover — the last factor in water reading. Learning to read water is learning to identify a place to fish. That place is likely to hold fish because all the fish attracting factors are present.

This develops into identifying better fish-holding areas which are more likely to hold fish than a lesser holding area. The better spots are more likely to hold bigger fish, because bigger fish dominate the best area by simply pushing smaller brethren out.

Tying it Together

Fishing success in the end comes from tying water reading together with lure presentation. The best way to get a lure right in against that root buttress that looks sure to hold a Murray cod is to use a sinking lure cast in tight and allowed to sink vertically by giving it slack line.

The best way to get a lure down along that horizontal tree trunk — where a bass should be laying up — is to run a deep diver beside it. The best way to fish a rock outcrop in a dam — which looks a likely holding place for golden perch and Murray cod — may not be to cast at all but to troll. Perhaps an echo sounder will help to determine the exact depth, or perhaps letting the lure back until it starts to bump the bottom will suffice.

Jiggling a tiny bladed spinner in an eddy area where silver perch should be is an effective presentation, because the flicking and

fluttering of the lure as the rod tip is twitched and lowered allowing the lure to sink, keeps the lure in the area where the silvers are likely to be. It also allows every level from the surface to the bottom to be probed — a potentially far more effective presentation than simply cranking the same lure through the same area.

Features of the Lure

The physical features of a lure also play an important role in selection and presentation. That bladed spinner is noisy and flashy.

A deep runner's long bib is perhaps equally as valuable an attribute as its ability to dive deeply. Long bibs 'trip' over obstructions making snagging unlikely and thus may be fished with some impunity over a boulder bottom and even among tree limbs.

Sinking shallow running lures are easier to snag up, but are best of all for placement tight against cover. They also respond to light touches of the rod tip and may be wiggled enticingly very close to cover — of vital importance when conditions aren't quite right and fish almost have to be 'hit' on the nose to entice a strike.

Deep divers are used too much by many people in this situation. By comparison, to make a deep diver plunge down it must be retrieved, which moves it away from the cover. At best, only minimal time is spent in the strike zone, at worst, it may pass outside the strike zone altogether and even though it's seen, no reaction will be forthcoming.

Many a top freshwater lure fisher has been moved to comment that ''the easy part comes after the strike''.

Lure fishing for freshwater natives is not the easiest form of fishing in this country. Gaining a strike at all — except for those 'flukey' times — is a matter of knowing the habits of the target fish, being able to determine where and when that fish will be in a position to be shown a lure, knowing lures well enough to choose one for a correct presentation and having the physical skills to make the presentation.

Not easy, but one of the most challenging and rewarding forms of fishing we have!

SEEKING OUT BASS STREAMS

Finding Our Bronzed Bombshell

The bass is one of Australia's most popular freshwater sportfish. Aggressive by nature, bass can be quick to hit a lure or bait. But the most difficult step for a would-be bass angler is locating a stream that holds good numbers of these fish.

These days the odds are long against experienced bass fishermen revealing the whereabouts of their favourite streams. Like jungle perch in the tropics, the range of bass is diminishing and anglers are growing increasingly secretive about their haunts. Besides, you will gain more satisfaction by discovering your own streams.

There are ways to find such streams. The best scheme is to consider all the conditions that are necessary for bass to maintain a large, healthy population. Then examine a number of waterways until you find those that best meet the needs. These are the streams you should fish.

ABOVE: A canoe and lightweight punt trolling slowly into some likely bass water on a misty morning. Although most bass are caught casting and retrieving, trolling deep-running plugs can be a reasonable method of prospecting new water.

This will mean getting out and examining rivers and creeks, and though this can involve a lot of hard slogging through rough country, your first strike from one of those big 'bronzed battlers' will instantly make it all worthwhile. To find the elusive first fish there are a number of points you should consider. These include: the geographic range of bass; the type of streams they prefer; the factors affecting their distribution within a particular stream; how to locate suitable streams; the time of year when bass are most abundant; and the best methods of inducing bass to take a lure.

Distribution and Behaviour

Australian bass occur in the small streams entering Tin Can Bay in southern Queensland and throughout the coastal creeks and rivers of New South Wales and south at least to Wilson's Promontory in Victoria.

For most of this range, south from the Richmond River, the bass (*Macquaria novaemaculatus*) overlaps with the very similar, yet separate, species of fish known as estuary perch (*Macquaria colonorum*). These estuary perch are confined to salt or brackish water, and will take lures. It hardly matters which of the two species you hook; both fight equally well.

Bass are strange fish. Their ancestors were marine fish that slowly colonised freshwater. But they maintained their links with the sea to the extent that even today bass must return to salt water, or even brackish water, in order to spawn. In freshwater their eggs cannot be fertilised. Therefore bass can only maintain a constant population in a stream where they have access to the sea. Adult and newly-hatched fish alike will swim into the very top reaches of a stream to feed and grow, but when they feel the spawning urge they will migrate to the estuaries.

So what you are looking for is a stream that runs from the Great Dividing Range east into the sea. There are no bass in the Murray-Darling river system. (Although a few estuary perch have been recorded from the mouth of the Murray River in South Australia.)

Bass generally spawn during winter and spring and use the floods of spring-summer to move back upstream. Though the swirling floodwaters of the east coast rivers might seem far too strong for any fish, there is usually a narrow 'gutter' of still, or even back-eddying, water very close to the banks that can help fish work their way upstream.

When these floods blur the usual contours of the river and submerge normally dry ground, bass can find their way into very strange places. Even old stump holes or farmers' dams kilometres from the river's normal course might hold bass if the area has been inundated by rising waters. So don't overlook lagoons and small lakes, even though they might not be joined to a stream at the time. As long as they are joined to an east coast stream at least once every few years mature fish will find their way out to spawn downstream and fingerlings find their way in to maintain the population. In fact small pools cut off for several years have been known to hold a few very large bass, and the angler should not overlook these pockets of water.

Limiting Influences

Many factors affect the distribution of bass in a particular stream. In normal conditions bass will move upstream as far as the first insurmountable barrier. For instance, many experienced bass anglers will follow a stream on

> 'Small pools cut off for several years have been known to hold a few very large bass, and the angler should not overlook these pockets of water.'

RELEASING FISH

When you have landed a bass, what to do with it is up to you. Bass can be delicious to eat, especially if cooked in the coals of a campfire by the stream where they were caught. No one should miss the special delights of eating a freshly caught bass.

These days growing numbers of anglers are releasing bass due to declining stocks. The easiest way to release the fish is to squeeze flat the barbs on the hooks before the trip. Then the hook can be easily slipped out of the fish's jaw without excessive handling.

Releasing any fish is a personal decision that should be made by each individual angler without pressure. But after the early rush of blood, most bass fishermen tend to free all but one or two fish.

Protection of bass, through bag limits, tighter fishing restrictions and proper management of waterways is being strengthened by fisheries authorities. Check with your nearest fishing inspector to make sure you are aware of the current regulations regarding bass.

foot or by canoe until they find a high waterfall or some other natural insurmountable obstacle and unless this has been overwhelmed by floodwaters, allowing bass to move on, the pool beneath it should hold bass. This is a feature experienced bass anglers seek.

Severe bushfires may deposit large quantities of ash in the water. This can choke a small creek and either kill the marine life or drive species downstream. Otherwise ideal bass streams in bushfire-prone regions can be ruined for fishing by this natural pollution. Local residents and emergency or bushfire services can tell you when a particular area last suffered major fires.

Man has also had a severe impact on bass. Some streams close to major centres of population have been seriously polluted and others have been heavily fished. Like most fish, bass are sensitive to pollution and this will either severely reduce their numbers or eliminate the species from some sections of the river altogether. And because bass are forced to travel from the very top of a stream to spawn they will be affected by pollution in any section downstream.

Illegal Netting

Heavy rod and line fishing certainly can reduce bass numbers, and possibly make the surviving fish 'lure shy'. However it is unlikely this fishing technique alone can make severe inroads on a river's population. What does have a very serious affect is illegal netting. Gill nets set along coastal rivers illegally can take large numbers of bass, especially when they are moving in large numbers at spawning time. At such times netting removes the very fish that by spawning would ensure the future survival of bass in good numbers in that particular waterway.

Remote Streams

These are two reasons why experienced anglers prefer to search out streams as far as possible from major population centres. Though bass are sometimes caught close to large cities, within the suburbs of Brisbane and the southern suburbs of Sydney, for instance, the chances of catching fish are higher in more remote areas.

ABOVE: An experienced bass fisherman leads a played-out fish to his punt prior to releasing it. BOTTOM: This canoe fisherman is working a quiet, snag-studded backwater on a river not far from Sydney.

'Experienced anglers prefer to search out streams as far as possible from major population centres.'

TOP: Smaller streams such as this can produce some superb bass fishing, especially in areas with relatively little pollution and limited people pressure.
ABOVE: More and more anglers are turning to the fly rod for bass. The species responds well to small, cork-bodied popping flies such as this.

Man's work as an engineer also seriously encroaches upon the habitat of bass. High dams, for instance, seriously affect their migratory movements. Bass returning from the downstream spawning run cannot of course climb over dam walls and so are packed into the creek or river below the wall. Gradually the waters above the dam wall will become depopulated as bass go over the spillway during floods, are killed in screens or turbines in low-level water intakes, or just die of old age.

Streams with high dams on them can still provide excellent bass fishing, but only downstream of the wall, and the river overall will hold fewer fish and in a smaller area than it did before the dam was built. The exception, of course, is where hatchery-bred bass are stocked above the dam.

Other changes to the waterways also affect bass, though not always as obvious as high dams. Many once rewarding bass streams have been ruined by silt. Like most native fish, bass prefer deep and sheltered holes. The cutting down of stream-side vegetation, planting of crops too close to the water's edge, and the trampling of grass and destruction of young trees by cattle and other domestic animals have caused serious erosion. Soil and gravel washed from the destabilised banks have filled many deeper streams and left instead shallow, sandy drains that can support very few fish.

It is understandable why keen bass anglers seek out the less disturbed streams, particularly those that flow for most of their length through thick forest or steep, rocky country too rough to farm. However, some of the rich, dairy country creeks and rivers should not be overlooked as good bass territory. In some of these areas the banks are still fairly well protected and bass can still be caught in the deeper sections.

It has already been stated that downstream changes also affect bass. In some areas development of canal estates or industrialisation will have meant removal of mangrove or other natural estuarine shelter for juvenile fish. Lacking proper food and shelter, small bass are less likely to survive, and so the entire stream will contain fewer fish.

These are all very important points to remember when searching for your ideal stream.

Read Maps for Information

The starting point should always be a map. Contour maps provide wonderful information once you have mastered the task of reading them. For instance, you can pick the steep country unlikely to carry crops, the heavily forested land still safe from erosion, the slow-winding, probably deep streams yet to be dammed. These maps will also show the trails that will take a four-wheel drive vehicle or old bridle paths that are at least negotiable on foot.

Decide how far you are prepared to travel away from home and buy maps to cover the region. Begin with the 1:250 000 series for a broad coverage of the area and then focus on particular spots with a 1:50 000 map. Check also to see when these maps were last updated and consult the forestry people or local shire councils for information regarding any changes to the rivers and roads in the area since that time.

Field Work Necessary

Having selected a particular stream for closer inspection some field work is necessary. If you have the time it is a good idea to cover the entire stream from mouth to source. This is rarely practical or possible, but it is a terrific advantage when bass fishing to know what's round the next bend in the stream.

The best bass streams will not have many access points by road. You may have to canoe upstream from the lower reaches, or walk in and inspect it on foot; an inflatable rubber canoe is a valuable aid provided it is light enough to backpack.

Though this might sound to the uninitiated a little like a fisherman's tale, there is a great deal of very valuable information to be gleaned in country pubs. They are well worth visiting on a Saturday afternoon. This is when the local farmers might get together for a quiet drink, and from time to time you might find the conversation turns to fishing. Many country people are surprisingly open and don't mind steering a friendly stranger towards a reliable fishing hole. It might not be the best spot they know, but it is sure to hold at least a few fish. Repay their courtesy by keeping the spot to yourself and leaving it the way you found it. Then you'll be equally welcome next time.

It is also an excellent opportunity to talk to the locals about access. The quickest way to many streams is often through private property. Landowners feel the same way about someone crossing their paddocks as city folk do about people shortcutting through their backyards. Always ask permission first, and don't forget to ask how the 'perch' are biting. Few country people call them bass.

Best Times to Fish

Bass are best known as summer fish. During the cooler months they are usually downstream around the spawning areas and can be hard to find. In the warmer weather they

move back upstream and stir into active feeding again.

In Queensland it is thought that bass spawn during the months of June and July. In Victoria they seem to spawn later, from September onwards. After spawning the fish are hungry and their return upstream coincides with an increase in insect life with the warmer days.

The fishing can be particularly good when insects like cicadas and crickets take to the air. Many of them end up in the water and bass are quick to snatch any insect struggling on the surface. (For that matter, they will take mice, lizards and small birds as well.)

Towards the northern end of their range, it is common to hear fishermen say bass can be caught during any month with an 'R' in it; that is, September to April. However further south the earlier frosts and longer winters seem to shorten the period of intense activity by bass. Keen anglers in this area still do fish for bass well into winter, though they will often concentrate on the evening periods after sunny days have warmed the water.

Generally speaking, the nearer it is to the middle of summer the further upstream you can expect to find fish; the nearer it is to mid-winter the further downstream you should search. This will be affected by varying seasonal conditions; with heavy rains just prior to the spawning season bass will have to move further downstream to find water of sufficient salinity for spawning, and conversely during drought periods when salt water moves further upstream they will not need to migrate so far. With flood rains immediately after the spawning season they will travel further upstream and gain access to the top reaches and otherwise isolated lagoons earlier than usual.

ABOVE: In rugged country the bass angler must travel light. This small but well-stocked kit of lures contains just enough hardware to cover most options. Note the metal-winged Crazy Crawler in the right-hand side of the box. These are excellent surface lures for bass.

'The cutting down of streamside vegetation, planting of crops too close to the water's edge, and the trampling of grass and destruction of young trees by cattle and other domestic animals have caused serious erosion.'

Reading a Stream

The instinct of bass is to lie under cover, and they are rarely seen during daylight in open water, unlike trout. They have a distinct preference for live food, especially small fish, prawns, insects and yabbies. During the day, rather than hunt actively for their prey, bass usually prefer to strike from ambush. Snags such as fallen trees, sunken logs, roots, rocks and undercut banks are favourite hangouts. Casting to these features is likely to find a bass.

Bass are usually found close to the bank rather than in open water, particularly during the day. This is where they find the most shelter. During the cooler, shadier periods of early morning and late afternoon, and especially at night, bass will move out, particularly into weed beds, even quite shallow ones, to search for shrimp and other favourite food.

Fish are often located at the head of a pool, particularly during the early summer. In their natural migration upstream, fish may tend to concentrate at the heads of pools, awaiting a sufficient flow of water or the cover of darkness to swim through shallows or rapids and into the next major hole.

The head of a pool is also often the spot that will hold the biggest fish. Where rapids enter quieter water is a choice feeding spot and the bigger bass possibly take up this site to catch the food carried into the pool. Whatever the reason, the first deep, sheltered water below a rapid or shallow run has produced numerous big bass for many fishermen.

TOP: The Macleay River — seen here flowing into Kempsey, northern NSW — is a justifiably renowned bass water, though stocks have declined in recent years.
ABOVE: An adult cicada — top bass tucker!
ABOVE RIGHT: This fat female came from the Shoalhaven River in southern NSW.

Selection of Lures

Novice fishermen sometimes agonise over the selection of lures for bass. They spend hours experimenting to see which common commercial lures will take bass. In later life they will probably spend even more hours experimenting to see which common, and uncommon, lures will not deceive bass. Bass will hit almost anything that resembles a struggling animal. Remember that in the quieter streams most fish will never have seen a lure; anything that flutters or splutters is to them food. Bass have been known to hit twigs twitched across the surface.

However, there are a number of lures which are very popular with bass fishermen. These include the Flopy, Nilsmaster and Rebel Halfback minnows, and Crazy Crawler and Jitterbug surface poppers. Some anglers are also using bulky trout flies like the Mrs Simpson and Muddler Minnow with astonishing success.

Bass definitely feed more actively in the early morning, late afternoon and evening, but they can be caught during the heat of the day. These fish tend to feed nearer the river bed during the day, rising to search for insects and other terrestrial animals that might have found themselves in the water momentarily. Bass will sometimes follow the flight of insects over the water and hit them as soon as they land; they can do the same with lures.

Working the Lure

Bass are attracted by movement, particularly movement suggesting their prey is weak or injured. This accounts for the need to apply some degree of skill in working a lure to attract a strike. The classic retrieve is the 'wounded flutter'. Cast the lure, let it lie until the ripples have smoothed away, then give it a kick, let it lie, give it another kick, let it lie for a shorter period; let it lie, kick it again, then slowly draw it in, giving an occasional kick or flutter as it comes. If this doesn't draw a strike, stop the lure again midway during the retrieve, let all the ripples die away, give one small, sharp kick, and retrieve the lure more quickly. Faced with the possibility of its 'victim' escaping back to dry land, an uncertain bass might be finally drawn into a strike. Try different types of retrieve actions until you find the one the bass like best.

One thing you need in any type of fishing, but bass fishing in particular, is confidence. You have to believe in yourself, in your choice of stream and snag, and in your lure. You can catch a bass, you can catch a bass in this creek under this log, and you can catch a bass with this lure. Believing all that, you will cast the lure to that snag time and time again. And eventually you will catch a bass!

Experienced bass fishermen will anchor their boats and cast repeatedly to one snag for up to 20 minutes. Then they might cast for 10 minutes more. If they catch small bass they will release them and continue casting. Often they will be rewarded by a bragging-size bass.

One of these days you are going to paddle quietly into the soft light of late afternoon and suddenly all round you bass are going to be hitting surface prey like a string of bombs. They will be frenzied and every cast will be snatched before the ripples spread. But it won't happen often.

Usually the bass have to be drawn out. They strike for two reasons: hunger or anger. If a bass is really hungry it will probably hit the lure on the first cast or soon after. If it is not, you then have to stir its territorial instincts. Keep casting that impudent lure and swim the lure through the bass's territory until the bass powers out to swallow it or chase it away.

After every bass trip, keep a record of conditions, results and locations. What time of the year was it, had there been any rain, what was the temperature, how many fish did you catch, what type of lures did they hit, what were the favourite colours? In this way you will have the formula for taking good bass and, just as important, where to take them.

TOP: Gripping a bass by its lower jaw allows the fish to be de-hooked and released with little chance of injury.

ABOVE: A trio of fine bass kept for the table. While there is nothing wrong with doing this occasionally, most thinking bass anglers these days choose to put them back.

A FLY FISHING PRIMER

Getting Started in the Noble Art

Bill Bachman/A.N.T. Photo Library

Some people are deterred by the supposed 'mystique' of fly fishing. However, gearing up for fly angling is no more daunting than preparing for any other style of fishing.

There he is, wading knee deep in the bubbling water of the mountain stream, line looping gracefully back and forth before shooting out above the water to deposit the fly gently on the surface. A lucky observer might see the fly vanish in a swirl and the angler flick the rod up in a quick strike, to be rewarded by a flash of silver as a trout leaps into the air and fights furiously on the end of the line.

It looks such a pleasant thing to be doing — such an enjoyable way to fish — that many people feel an irresistible urge to try it themselves.

Starting Out

Getting started in fly fishing for trout has never been easier. Today there are professional guides available who will not only take their clients to good places, but provide them with all the gear as well as teach them to use it properly. There is no doubt that this is the quickest way for someone to discover whether or not they have any affinity for the sport. It costs money, but on the other hand it saves spending heaps on fly fishing tackle which may be wasted. Fly fishing does not appeal to everyone; sometimes even those

ABOVE: The delightful world of fly fishing appeals to more and more people each year. Sadly, many are turned away by the misconception that this form of angling is extremely difficult and complicated. In truth, fly fishing can be mastered by anyone who can hold a rod.

ABOVE: A trio of fat, fit rainbow trout taken on a No 7 outfit rigged with a floating line.
BELOW: Master Kiwi fly fisher, Gary Kemsley, nets a hen rainbow of the size most visiting Aussies dream of catching.

who begin full of enthusiasm are disappointed.

Productive Method

The fact is, fly fishing is a very effective method of catching trout — some would say the **most** effective method — but beginners cannot expect to achieve high levels of skill without investing considerable time and effort.

Early attempts are likely to produce meagre results, so it is easy to understand why many decide to give up. However, fly fishing is a great sport, and gives enormous pleasure to millions of people all over the world.

An insight into the world of fly fishing can be gained from some of the excellent videos currently available. The best of these are very useful instructional tools, but also communicate the more abstract feelings associated with the sport. Whether it is Gary Borger shouting with excitement as a big trout takes him downstream on the mighty Madison River, or Mel Krieger explaining the philosophy of catch and release fishing, the messages come across clearly.

Pick a Shop

When it comes to gearing up to go fly fishing for trout, the first step is to find a good tackle shop.

Most places selling fishing equipment stock some items of fly fishing tackle, but because

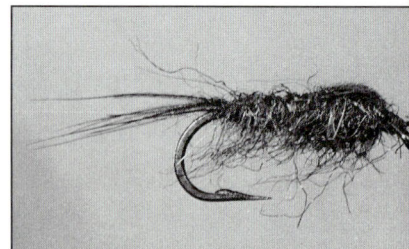

ABOVE: A couple of basic but effective fly patterns ideally suited to Australian lakes and streams. The top fly is a nymph, while the lower pattern is a wet. Note the flattened barbs on the hooks. This is to facilitate easy release of fish.

'Normal river trout fishing is covered by line weights No 5 and 6.

BELOW: You don't need to spend a fortune gearing up with fly tackle. An outfit such as this could be purchased for well under $200.
BOTTOM: The angler's grip while casting and fishing should be comfortable rather than rigidly adhering to those shown in text books.

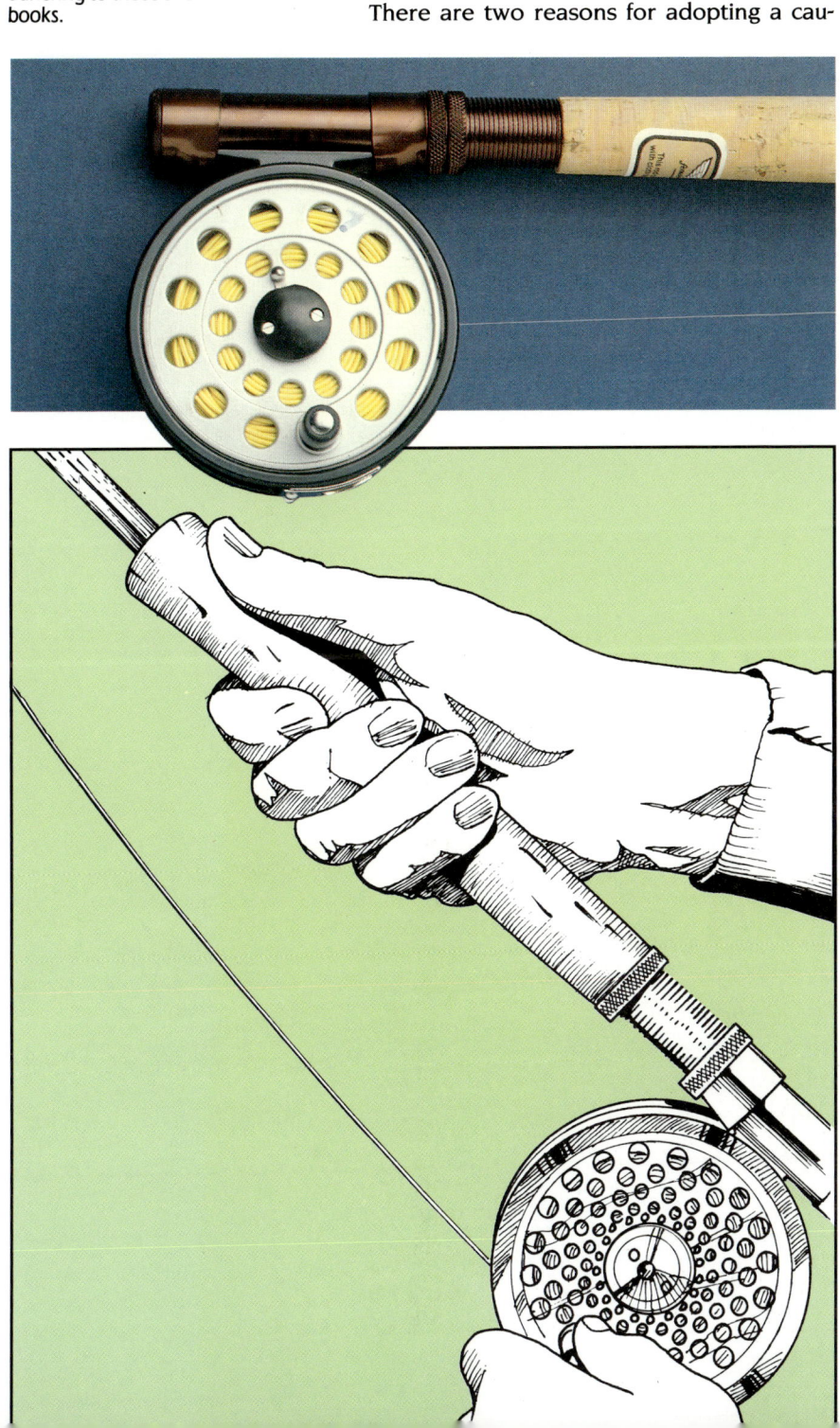

fly fishing is quite different from any other fishing method, it is well worth seeking out the specialist stores. These will have a much larger range of fly fishing gear and, more importantly, will be run by people who are themselves keen fly fishers. Here, the beginner will find a wider choice of tackle and someone with the knowledge to help them make the right selections.

For almost every item of fly fishing tackle, ancillary equipment, and clothing, there is a selection available which extends over an enormous price range.

It is not at all unusual for higher priced articles to be 10 times more expensive than cheaper alternatives.

In general, price reflects quality, and the expensive stuff is usually better. However, there are good reasons for not spending too much on first purchases.

There are two reasons for adopting a cautious approach in the beginning. For a start, many of the very desirable qualities possessed by higher priced items will go unnoticed or not be used by the newcomer to the sport. Only with growing confidence and skill will they be appreciated. Secondly, by the time this stage has been reached, the angler will have developed some particular tastes, and tackle purchased earlier may no longer meet these newly discovered requirements.

Mind you, it is not a good idea to buy the cheapest tackle, either. Learning to cast with fly fishing equipment is reasonably difficult without adding the handicap of inferior products. The best advice is to select from mid-priced items.

What to Buy

As well as a wide price range, fly fishing tackle also extends over a wide choice based on weight and power. There are ultra-light outfits for fishing small flies on small streams, and others with sufficient power to cast big, heavy flies over long distances.

Most artificial flies are very light in weight, and in casting, the rod is bent or loaded by the weight of the line, not the fly. It is the line which is cast; the fly simply going along for the ride.

Heavier flies require heavy lines to enable them to be cast properly. When flies are weighted a great deal to sink well in very fast water, a point is reached where the fly becomes too heavy for the line. This gives rise to the practice of 'chuck and duck' casting on big rivers such as the Tongarriro in New Zealand.

Before buying a rod it is necessary to decide what weight of line is to be used, and this, in turn, is determined by the kind of fishing.

Line weights No 3 and 4 are used in situations where a delicate presentation of the fly is paramount, as in trying to catch rising trout in smooth water. Normal casts will cover 10 to 15 metres, flies will be smaller than size 10, and strong winds will cause accuracy problems — to say the least.

Normal river trout fishing is covered by line weights No 5 and 6. These are light enough to give reasonable finesse, while also being able to handle reasonably windy weather and unweighted flies up to size 6, or smaller flies with added weight, as well as casting distances up to 25 metres or so.

By the time the heavier No 7 and 8 weight lines are in use, presentation of flies has been compromised in favour of power. This is the tackle usually associated with lake fishing or use in big rivers.

In some places, even heavier No 9 and 10 weight tackle is used for trout, but this is really getting into saltwater or salmon fishing territory, and doesn't have much place on the Australian scene.

Heavyweight lines are chosen partly for the ability to make long casts of 40 metres or more, and partly because — in the fast sinking types of line — the sink rate is much quicker.

Usual advice to beginners is to go for No 6 weight tackle. This is suitable for fishing rivers and streams, yet is powerful enough to give reasonable distance when trying lakes from the bank. Anything heavier, while it might make longer casting easier to learn, is a definite drawback in river fishing, where rising trout may be encountered.

Rods are often marked with two or even three line sizes which they can handle. One marked for 5/6 weight lines will have a crisper, faster action with a No 5 line, while being slower and easier to flex with a No 6 weight. In addition, rods are designed with different actions; their speed of flexing depending on their shape and the modulus of the material used in their construction. People who are quick movers usually prefer faster rods, while laid back types are better suited to slower actions.

Rod Materials

All fly rods in the middle price range are built of graphite, or graphite composites with boron or kevlar. Glass fibre has nothing much to offer these days, and only a few people are attracted to traditional split cane rods.

For some reason, rods are still mostly measured in feet. Anywhere between 8 and 9 feet is correct rod length for beginners.

Fly reels are mainly single action, meaning they have no gears, and are usually fitted with only a simple pawl and spring to function as a drag.

Some anglers prefer those that have a proper drag system as well as the click, and also favour models with an exposed spool rim so that they can jam a hand against it when things get really desperate.

Larger capacity reels sometimes have gearing, but these are not in the beginner's shopping list.

So that a second fly line may be used, it is a good idea to buy a spare spool for the reel.

Many of the reels available are made from metal or alloy and are rather heavy when mounted on the typical modern graphite rod. There are small metal reels which overcome this problem quite well, although they have limited line capacity, or there are reels made from lighter material, including magnesium and graphite.

In this country, it is unlikely that trout will be encountered that are going to strip off 100 metres or more of line and backing, so there is nothing to be gained from buying large capacity reels.

Fly Lines

The cost of fly lines never fails to shock newcomers. They are constructed by coating a central core of fibre, often nylon, with a plastic material. This plastic contains tiny glass bubbles if the line is to float, or lead dust if it is to sink.

The lines are tapered so that they will turn over smoothly at the end of each cast. They

ABOVE: An idyllic scene! Even if you're not a champion caster, it's great just being there.
BELOW: A competent fly fisher shoots a tight loop into some fast water on the Geehi River, NSW.
OPPOSITE CENTRE: Success!
OPPOSITE BOTTOM: Profile of a Kiwi rainbow.

come in a variety of shapes and densities. The range is confusing, to say the least.

Line weights have been explained already. A No 6 weight double taper floating line is the one for a beginner to choose for river trout fishing. A floating line is suitable for both dry and wet flies. A double tapered line has a taper at each end. This allows the line to be reversed when one end wears out, which is definitely worthwhile, especially when line wear will be high while learning to cast.

If it is intended to fish lakes as well as rivers, a second line which sinks will be found useful. When fishing wet flies on a floating line, the retrieve must be dead slow if the fly is not to be pulled up to the water's surface. This is fine for most river wet fly work, but in lakes it is often desired to retrieve wets with a faster action. On the other hand, sinking line stays down deep during even a fast retrieve.

Because this sinking line is intended mainly for lake fishing, it may be worth considering a

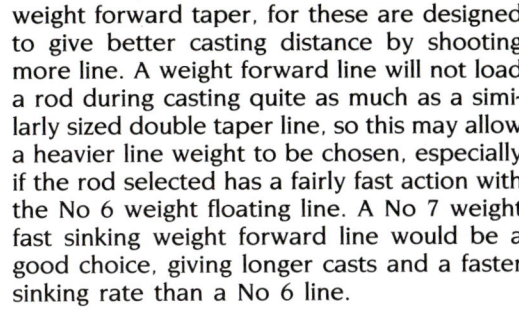

weight forward taper, for these are designed to give better casting distance by shooting more line. A weight forward line will not load a rod during casting quite as much as a similarly sized double taper line, so this may allow a heavier line weight to be chosen, especially if the rod selected has a fairly fast action with the No 6 weight floating line. A No 7 weight fast sinking weight forward line would be a good choice, giving longer casts and a faster sinking rate than a No 6 line.

Terminals

Now we're getting down to the business end of things. Before a fly can be cast to a trout, a leader must be attached to the end of the fly line.

The leader will be tapered, to continue the smooth turnover of the line, with a fine tippet to allow the fly to behave as if it is unattached, and about 3 metres long to keep the thick fly line away from the trout.

Leaders are measured in X's. A 4X and 5X will be most useful on rivers with flies in the size range 10 to 16, while for larger lake flies, a 3X may be needed.

After some use and several changes of fly, leaders will be shorter and thicker in the tippet than they were when fresh from the packet. Carrying some spools of leader material in 4X and 5X will allow new tippets to be added when needed.

A selection of flies really requires a separate chapter or book, but it is best to keep things simple at first. Imitative fly patterns assume the angler knows what is being imitated and how that thing behaves when in the trout's vision.

Attractor flies work well enough in situations where the trout gets no chance to give them a close scrutiny.

'Buggy' looking flies, or general 'suggestors', are the best choice for beginners. They may not interest the trout selectively feeding during a mayfly hatch, but when nothing much seems to be happening, which is a lot of the time, they will often fool the fish into taking.

Flies are carried in a box, and the box goes into a shoulder bag or the pocket of a vest or coat together with dozens of other things, most of which are not essential.

Odds 'n' Ends

It's worth noting the value of polarizing sunglasses, dry fly floatant, line floatant, and line snippers. The list of things fly fishers like to wear or hang upon themselves seems endless, and only personal experience will enable an appropriate selection for each individual.

This chapter has been about getting started on trout fly fishing, and for most who begin it is a journey which lasts a lifetime. Learning the techniques of casting and fishing leads to fishing tactics; which require a knowledge of the trout and their habits, and the lives of the insects upon which trout feed. In turn, this introduces fly-tying, or at least fly selection . . . And so it goes on. Definitely addictive!

FLY LINES

As explained in this chapter, fly casting is quite different to other styles of casting in that it relies on the weight of the line rather than a sinker, lure or bait to provide the weight necessary to carry a nearly weightless artificial fly out over the water.

To this end, flyline is very thick and quite heavy — much more so than even the strongest monofilament line. Because such a thick line would 'spook' the fish if tied directly to the fly, a leader of lighter nylon is tied to the working end.

There are several types of fly line available for different needs. To begin with, fly line is available in a range of weights to suit different strength rods and fly sizes. Common fly lines used in this country range from ultra-light AFTMA (American Fishing Tackle Manufacturers Association) No 4 up to the very heavy AFTMA No 12 and No 13 lines used in saltwater fly fishing.

Secondly, the line may be either floating or sinking, depending on its density. This is indicated by the addition to the serial number of an F for floating and an S for sinking. (Note that some fly lines, called 'sink tips' sink at the working end but float at the end attached to the reel or backing.)

Thirdly, the taper of a fly line varies. This dictates the line's behaviour in the air during casting and also influences how far it can be cast. Tapers include level (L), double taper (DT), weight forward (WF) and a special, short, heavy line called a shooting head or shooting taper (SH or ST).

All of this information about a flyline is incorporated into the serial number printed on its packaging, so that the buyer knows a DT6F line is a double taper, No 6 floating line (ideal for stream trouting), while a WF10S is a weight forward, No 10 sinking line, a popular choice for intermediate saltwater work.

BAITS AND LURES

Whether it is a live morsel, or one of the many varieties of freshwater lures which represent natural baits, once you know which foods your target species fancies, you're well on the way to a top catch. This section features a comprehensive guide to selecting the best baits and lures.

KNOW YOUR FRESHWATER BAITS

Inland Temptations

Our inland and outback freshwater sportfish fall for some very peculiar offerings at times, but over the long run there's simply nothing better than a well presented live morsel that's both attractive and familiar to the target species.

Before an angler can expect any kind of success, whether fishing an inland river or the open sea, he must take a close look at the habitat and behaviour of the fish he intends to trap, before putting a bait on a hook.

Fish behaviour varies and is usually a reaction to its environment. When a trout rises to the surface of a stream to take a fly, it is responding to a behaviour pattern which must be understood before the fisherman can expect a hook-up.

It should also be understood that every living creature in an inland stream environment is inter-connected through the food chain. For example, the larvae of insects are preyed upon by frogs and beetles which in turn are preyed upon by fish.

Feeding Pattern

It's also important to know the feeding patterns of the fish; whether it's a day or night feeder; whether it prefers the still, backwaters of a river or turbulent, swift-running streams and whether it's finicky or not fussy in relation to food. All these factors have a bearing on the type of bait which should be presented.

Food availability is another aspect which affects a freshwater angler's ability to take fish. Overpopulation of fish in a given stream will result in fierce competition for food, just as too much of a good thing will make the fish indifferent.

When trout are taking myriad spent mayflies on the surface of the water, they will often ignore a floating artificial.

Opportunistic Feeders

The freshwater carp will sometimes eat just about anything offered including dough, cheese, sausage and even a piece of bark! Most freshwater fish are opportunistic feeders. In other words, they make a meal of what's available at any given time.

While there are many stories of freshwater fish taking such bizarre baits as pieces of bullock, parrot flesh, boiled eggs, rabbit, field mice and snake, like all creatures most fish have a preference for their natural food. These more conventional items invariably make the best baits.

There is very little commercial fishing bait suitable for freshwater fish. In any case, locally gathered live bait is always the best and usually results in superior catches.

Irresistible Baits

Some of the top natural baits which nearly all freshwater fish find irresistible include crickets, worms, grasshoppers, freshwater shrimp, worms, witchetty grubs, locusts, green frogs, insects, crustaceans, molluscs and other fish.

Just about any insect, both terrestrial and aquatic, will be taken by trout. Some of these creatures are too small to be placed on a hook, others are much too large. Many have been imitated by artificial flies.

The top natural baits for trout are crickets, beetles, shrimps, mudeyes (larvae of the dragonfly), grasshoppers and small grubs.

Worms

From yellowbelly and silver perch to bass and trout, worms are top bait for almost all inland fish. The easily-collected, common garden worm is often used while the highly active red worm, which never stops wriggling, is a well known fish taker.

Many dedicated freshwater anglers breed worms exclusively for their own bait. A sugar bag placed where it can be kept permanently damp in the backyard is a good spot to start a worm colony. A good supply of wrigglers will be found under the bag in no time, especially after wet weather.

Many anglers prefer to dig for worms at the river side near their favourite fishing spot, reasoning that the fish will be more likely to accept local worms.

Freshwater Shrimps

A freshwater crustacean similar to the saltwater prawn, the shrimp is considered by many freshwater anglers to be the most effective freshwater bait due to the fact that predatory fish will rarely reject them, particularly when used alive and kicking.

It's an easy matter to collect shrimp with a shrimp bucket: a specially designed drum or tin with holes punctured in the sides and

baited with meat or fish heads before being submerged.

Best spots to look for shrimps are close to the water's edge in the vicinity of aquatic weeds, near algae covered logs, bushes overhanging the stream and rocky patches where stream litter such as leaves and twigs have gathered.

Often a better haul can be made at night, when the shrimp are generally more active. Yabbies or freshwater crayfish will also be taken in these buckets at times.

Grubs

Long before white man cast a fishing line into an inland river, the Aboriginals were using witchetty grubs and other varieties to trap fish.

The 'bardi' or witchetty grub is an excellent bait for Murray cod, yellowbelly, catfish and other popular inland fish. They can be extracted from their holes around the base of large gum trees with a length of wire with a corkscrew end.

Other varieties of wood grubs can be dug up, chopped out of rotting timber or extracted from holes in willow, kurrajong and peppercorn trees. Healthy grubs will keep quite well in a glass jar with some bark or leaf litter.

Yabbies

Distinguished by their large claws, this family of freshwater crayfish represent a universal bait for freshwater fishing. At various stages of their growth, yabbies are eaten by all of our native fish. Larger specimens are a top bait for big Murray cod.

The traditional catching method often enjoyed by children is to trap them with a piece of meat on a length of string. More earnest fishermen often use a yabby rake, or rely on various pots, nets and baited traps similar to those used in saltwater to catch crabs.

Frogs

Many times when freshwater anglers run out of bait, they hook up a frog with good results. Frogs, like worms, are a popular food with many of our inland fish particularly

ABOVE: A freshwater shrimp — top bait for most outback species. OPPOSITE: Remote freshwater country such as this holds vast reserves of natural bait if the angler knows where to look.

'Most freshwater fish are opportunistic feeders — they make a meal of what's available.'

LEFT: Yabbies! Top tucker and even better bait. These freshwater crayfish are widespread through inland lakes, rivers, dams and waterholes.
BOTTOM: A simply made shrimp trap will produce plentiful live bait.

Australian Picture Library.

'Preparation and presentation of any bait is of the greatest importance.'

yellowbellow, cod and trout, and even barramundi and saratoga have been taken with a frog bait.

Frogs taken from those areas close to the stream to be fished are always preferred. Popular hiding spots are moist areas under rocks, logs and forest litter. The small, brown frog, often found near river gums seems to take more fish than green frogs.

Mussels

Often while dragging shallow river beds for yabbies, the freshwater angler will come across a supply of freshwater mussels, another good bait for inland fish.

For those who might consider making a meal of these molluscs, a word of advice. A cooked, freshwater mussel does not match its saltwater counterpart in taste and tenderness!

The flesh inside these molluscs, which can measure as much as 10 cm across, can be baited whole for large Murray cod or cut into strips for smaller fish. Freshwater mussels can be found partly exposed in the soft sediment of creeks, billabongs and rivers and can often be felt by the feet while wading.

A drawback of this bait is its appeal to the introduced pest fish, European carp.

ABOVE: The macrobrachium or freshwater prawn of tropical rivers is a superb barramundi bait.
BELOW: This grasshopper has been hooked lightly through the wings so that it will stay alive and kicking to tempt a trout, bass or sooty grunter.

Q & A

How good are the commercially made packet baits such as Catchit?

These manufactured baits cannot match the appeal of natural items over the longer run, but they certainly do have their days. Trout and carp, in particular, are regularly taken on small blobs of these packet baits, particularly in clouded or discoloured water following heavy rain.

What's the difference between a saltwater yabby and a freshwater yabby?

Apart from both being crustacea and both making excellent baits, these two creatures have little in common. The saltwater yabby, which is also called a bass yabby, pink nipper, ghost prawn or clicker, is a small pinkish white prawn-like creature with one oversized claw. It lives in burrows on tidal sandflats and is usually taken by anglers using a specially designed suction device called a yabby pump. On the other hand, the freshwater yabby — actually several different species — grows considerably larger than its marine counterpart, has two well developed claws, is usually brown, dark blue or black and can most readily be captured on a line baited with smelly meat or in a similarly baited trap.

Macrobrachium

These giant freshwater prawns are native to the northern rivers of the continent and are a useful bait for many tropical fish species. They are usually trapped at night when they are attracted to fish flesh baits in buckets or nets. However, they may also be taken during the day with a cast, scoop or drag net.

These long-legged shrimps are also delicious eating and a good haul often ends up on a fisherman's plate rather than being sacrificed as bait.

Freshwater prawns are excellent bait for barramundi and the many other freshwater fish found in our northern, tropical rivers.

Small Fish

Small, live fish are attractive baits for a number of species including trout, bass, Murray cod, golden perch, redfin and barramundi.

It's a good idea to check with your state regulations before using some fish such as carp and goldfish; it can be an offence to transport these fish from one waterway to another, or even to use them as bait. Similarly, live bait fishermen need to be aware of legal length restrictions on some species.

Little minnows, galaxia and gudgeon, gathered with a scoop net, are great baits for redfin and yellowbelly and many of the large predators will take both dead and live fish.

Miscellaneous Baits

It is true to say that most creatures that live in a river or fall into it are more than likely eaten by fish at some time. With this in mind, baits of crickets, beetles, grasshoppers, centipedes, spiders and moths can all be hooked up and tried as bait.

Trout and bass both relish grasshoppers, cicadas and crickets. Trout also appreciate most insects but a large portion of their diet are nymphs; mainly the larvae of various members of the mayfly families.

Preparation and presentation of any bait is of the greatest importance. It should look as natural as possible and be placed in the right position at the right time. The most successful inland angler is the one who knows the natural food of the fish he's seeking to trap and presents it in as lifelike a manner as possible.

FRESHWATER LURES

Outback Artificials

Freshwater lures represent all types of natural food, from worms and frogs to mice and small injured fish. These lures provide the freshwater angler with an exciting alternative for catching freshwater fish in our inland lake and river systems.

Whereas bait fishermen are confined to patiently staking out one particular stretch of river bank or inland impoundment, lure anglers can cover a surprisingly large area of water, particularly in the faster-flowing reaches of rivers and in hilly tableland regions.

The water in these areas is cleaner and better oxygenated than the sluggish and often heavily silted waters of the Murray-Darling system.

During times of peak activity, many of our freshwater fish will rise and take a surface popper, sometimes as soon as the lure has hit the surface. More commonly, lures need to be worked well under the water and down into the vicinity of feeding areas such as weed beds and submerged logs.

Although the old Aussie-made Aeroplane spinner remains a firm favourite with some inland anglers, and good sized fish are still landed on them, freshwater lures have come a long way in the past decade. Plugs such as the Flatfish and the Flopy also remain popular, but have been joined by a vast array of artificials from America and Europe, as well as several superbly made Australian products.

Barramundi

When barramundi are on the bite, they respond to an incredible range of lures, running the full gamut from lead head jigs to surface poppers. However, experienced barra fishermen swear by minnow-patterned, bibbed lures with a particular 'shimmy' or wiggle rather than the pronounced wobble.

Whatever lure is used, barramundi require sturdy tackle; over-strength hooks and split

OPPOSITE: This beautiful sooty grunter fell to a hand-crafted timber lure.
1 This Finnish-made Nilsmaster Stalwart has many freshwater applications.
2 A typical plug for bass, cod, perch and the like. This one's a Shakespeare Big S.
3 A range of topwater lures and poppers.
4 Deep diving plugs feature large bibs or swimming lips.
5 A redfin perch which fell for a small maribou-dressed Crappie Jig worked close to the bottom near a stand of drowned timber.

'Freshwater lures have come a long way in the past decade.'

TOP LEFT: The sooty grunter is a great tropical sportster. This one hit a Rapala Fat Rap plug.
LEFT: Spinning blade lures or spinners come in an assortment of shapes, sizes and colours.
BELOW: The beautiful and endangered jungle perch. Lure is a Rebel Crawdad.
TOP RIGHT: Large brown trout taken on a Jensen Insect spinner.
CENTRE RIGHT: Redfin and the Celta which tempted it.
BOTTOM RIGHT: This massive albino catfish took a Nilsmaster Invincible.

'Surface running plugs, poppers and "fizz baits" can be very effective, especially on warm evenings. '

rings and a wire or heavy nylon leader attached to the lure.

Many regular barramundi anglers have devised their own lures, but popular commercial models include imported Nilmaster, Rebel, Rapala and Cotton Cordell patterns, and Australian cottage industry products such as Killalures, Elliots, Leads Lures, C-Lures, Newell Scorpions and Nautilus Lures, to name just a few.

In very fast flowing water and during heavy monsoonal run-off, lead head rubber jigs like the Vibrotail, Scrounger and Mr Twister have proved their worth.

A relatively recent trend in barra fishing has seen great catches being taken with the bibless, sinking 'sonic' style of lure such as Cotton Cordell's Rattlin' Spot. These are especially successful when jigged up and down in close proximity to snags and other cover.

Bass

One of the most sought-after indigenous freshwater fish, Australian bass offer superb sport for the spin fisherman. They attack lures with gusto and fight strongly to avoid capture.

Much of the diet of the bass, especially in summer, consists of aquatic and terrestrial insects or their larvae. This means they can be tempted with a range of trout flies and lures. However, the most successful lures are American-style diving plugs or 'crank baits' with a built-in action which makes them dive and wobble when retrieved.

Floating-diving lures which float at rest but dive when retrieved are among the most efficient bass catchers.

Bass will often fall for quite large-bodied floating lures and many times the strike will come as soon as the lure hits the water. Similarly, surface running plugs, poppers and 'fizz baits' can be very effective, especially on warm evenings.

Murray Cod and Yellowbelly

In the long reaches of many inland rivers and across the wide areas of lakes and reservoirs, trolling with lures can be a highly profitable way of freshwater fishing.

As well as trout, many of our native sportfish including Murray cod and golden perch or yellowbelly can be taken this way.

Lures are particularly suitable for snaring Murray cod in the large inland dams, where working the areas around backwater spots holding stands of drowned timber, especially during the warmer months, is a good recipe for success. The fish become particularly active from about late August until early May.

Trolling behind a boat and working large lures by casting and retrieving around sections of dead timber has taken many dam-dwelling native fish.

Golden perch, also called yellowbelly or callop, will fall to a wide range of spinners, spoons and plugs. Bass lures and their larger stablemates work best.

Best bet is to work the lure deep around

logs, rock bars and weed beds. Areas immediately downstream of weirs or dams often provide better than average angling.

The Small Native Perches

Our outback Macquarie perch, silver perch and spangled perch, along with the sooty grunter and jungle perch of the tropic north, all respond to lures at times.

Best choices for most of these perch are based around the smaller bass lures, especially compact, deep diving plugs. However, spinners and spoons are also productive, particularly on silvers and spangled perch.

The tropic perches strike actively at surface lures when in the mood.

Trout

Although more purist trout anglers prefer to fish for trout with a specialised collection of dry and wet flies, these introduced sportfish often fall victim to an artificial lure imitating a frog, a small fish or an insect.

Metal spinners are the best bet and balance well with light threadline outfits.

Trout can be just as selective with spinners as they are with flies and often different types will need to be tried before an acceptable one is found. Popular spinning blade lures include the Celtas, Mepps, Vibrax, Gibbs and Jensens. Spoons such as the Australian Wonder Wobbler, Pegron Tiger Minnow and Tantangara spoon work well in larger bodies of water or more turbulent rivers.

Bibbed minnows such as Rapalas and Nilsmasters work well at times, as do tiny lead head jigs and streamer flies weighted with split shot. Trolling lures like the Baltic Minnow and Tasmanian Devil can be cast and retrieved, but are best pulled behind a slow moving boat.

One good method of spinning for trout is to cast upstream and retrieve a little faster than the flow of the river, so as to impart action to the lure.

For average to large trout, the popular Helin Flatfish and its many imitators will reap rewards when trolled. Most freshwater trollers use metal, plastic or wooden lures, but some prefer flies, particularly when weighted with split shot or lead core line.

Redfin Perch

The redfin or English perch is an introduced fish which although something of a pest, is popular with many freshwater lure fishermen.

These fish will take most small to medium freshwater lures, especially those fished near the bottom. Jigging with bobbers and small metal fish imitations works particularly well. They are also susceptible to a wet fly, especially to those with a streamer pattern.

Deep-diving wobblers and plugs, bladed spinners and metal spoons are all attractive to redfin, too. A straightforward cast and retrieve will often score, though sink 'n' draw retrieves and jigging add to the artificial's attractiveness.

FISH FACTS

Many freshwater fish rate among Australia's top sportsfish. This section explores the challenge of the trout, the ferocity of the bass and the might of the Murray Cod. It also includes chapters on golden perch and European carp.

TROUT 1

Speckled Aristocrats of the Sweetwater

Few fish play a bigger part than trout in the history and folklore of fishing throughout the world, and no other species enjoys such a keen following among freshwater anglers. Since their successful introduction to Australia last century, trout have carved themselves a permanent place as a premier sportfish.

Visitors to Australia are often surprised to learn that such a dry continent boasts some of the world's best and most readily accessible trout fishing. This situation is made all the more incongruous by the fact that trout are native to the cooler regions of the northern hemisphere and were completely unknown south of the equator until the second half of the last century!

The first trout to be introduced to Australasian waters were brown trout (*Salmo trutta*), which were shipped from Britain in 1864. Four years later, progeny of these successfully acclimatised browns were transported to New Zealand, where they quickly established themselves in that country's many cold, clean streams and lakes.

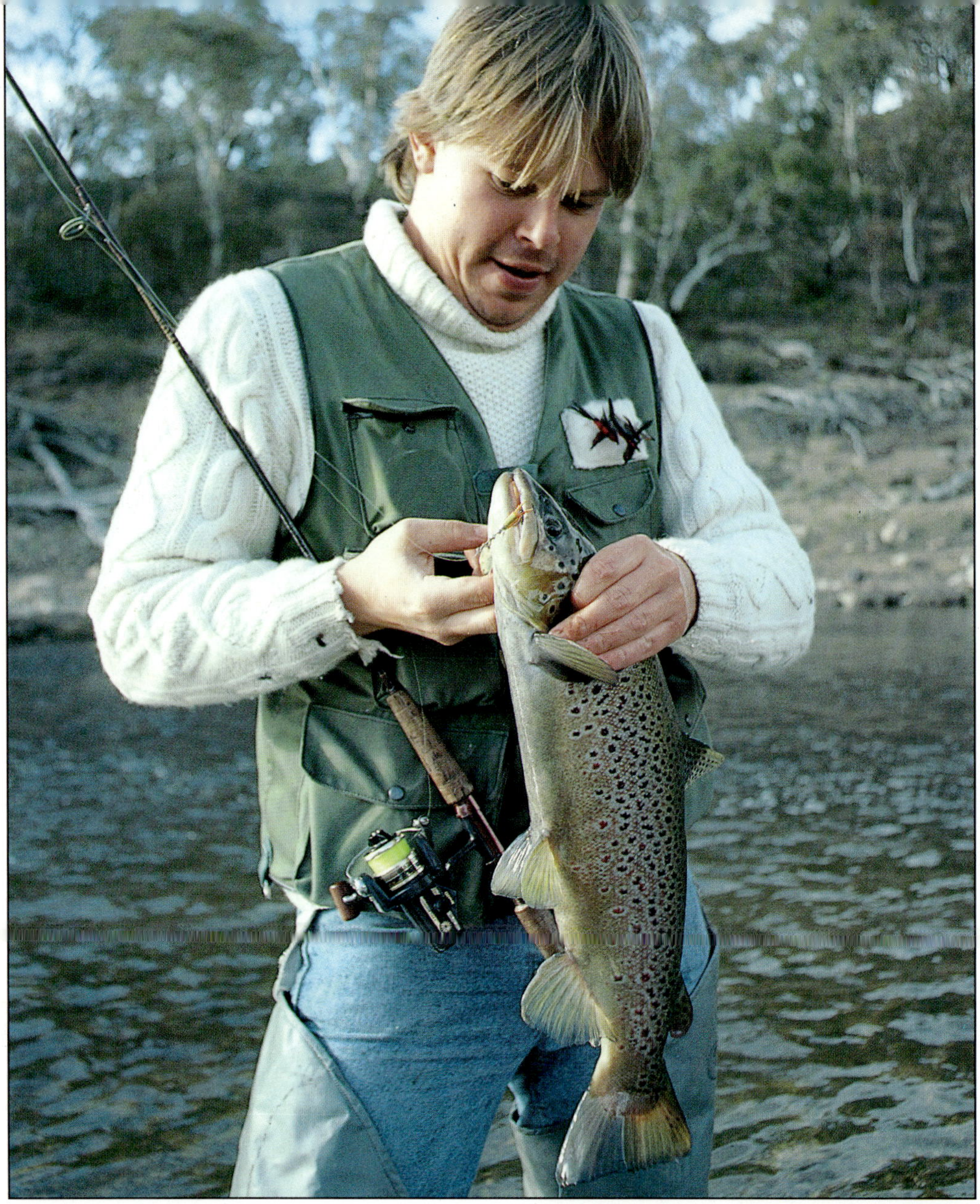

'Healthy populations of trout are to be found in New South Wales, Victoria, Tasmania, South Australia, the southern corner of Western Australia and in the Australian Capital Territory.'

LEFT: A beautiful 2.5 kg brown trout from the Thredbo River in southern New South Wales.
BELOW: Brown trout have adapted to a wider range of environments than other introduced salmonoids.
OPPOSITE: There's more to trout fishing than catching trout!

Other members of the family *Salmonidae*, which encompasses most of the trout and 'true' salmon, were stocked in Australian waters throughout the latter years of the 19th century, but none met with the same long term success as brown trout until the introduction of stocks of colourful North American rainbow trout (*Salmo gairdneri*) during the early 1900s.

Today, practically all trout caught in Australia are descendants of those original liberations of brown and rainbow trout, although pockets of brook trout (*Salvelinus fontinalis*), Atlantic salmon (*Salmo salar*) and chinook or 'quinnat' salmon (*Oncorhynchus tshawytscha*) do exist in some states. For practical purposes, however, trout fishing in Australia is all about the capture of just two species: the wily, aristocratic European brown, and the brash, aggressive American rainbow.

Trout in Australia

Today, healthy populations of trout are to be found in New South Wales, Victoria, Tasmania, South Australia, the southern corner of

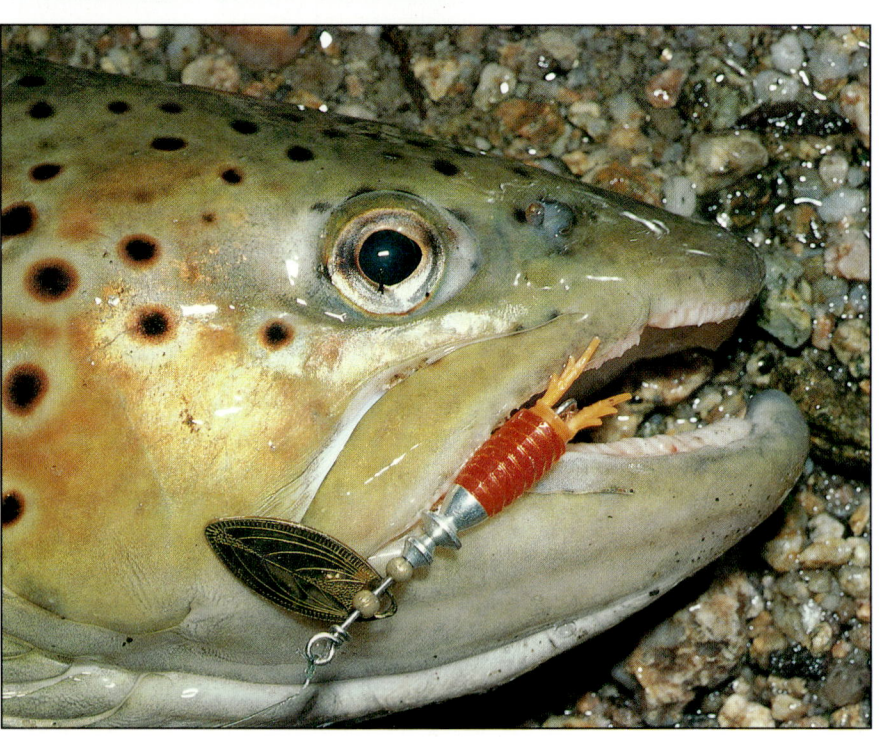

'Australia boasts some superb, self-sustaining trout fisheries.'

Western Australia and in the Australian Capital Territory. Introductions of these fish to the southern interior of Queensland have so far proven unsuccessful.

Trout originally evolved in the cooler regions of the northern hemisphere. As a result of their evolutionary origins, they thrive in cold, unpolluted and well oxygenated water, and although it appears that subsequent generations of 'migrant' trout in Australia have adapted a little to the harsh climate, they do not prosper in the very warm, turbid conditions which suit Australia's native freshwater fishes.

Of the two species which dominate the Australian trout fishery, browns have proven the more adaptable and hardy and have therefore colonised a wider range of aquatic environments. Rainbows, on the other hand, remain more restricted in their distribution as a result of their limited tolerance to high temperatures and low oxygen levels. Browns will survive briefly at temperatures as high as 28 degrees Celsius, while rainbows become extremely distressed and eventually die in water much warmer than about 21 degrees Celsius. Both species do best and grow fastest within a temperature range of approximately 10 to 20 degrees Celsius.

BELOW: Netting a big, male rainbow trout in brightly-hued pre-spawning coloration.

Re-stocked or Self-sustaining?

The mere survival of trout should not be confused with the successful establishment of self-sustaining populations. The majority of mainland Australian trout waters must be regarded as 'marginal' in that worthwhile populations are only maintained over the longer term by repeated re-stocking with hatchery bred fry and fingerlings, as well as the occasional liberations of adult brood stock in some areas. Trout have quite specific spawning requirements based around the need for cold, running water and beds of clean gravel made up of pebbles within a particular size range. For these reasons, many Australian streams and lakes offer only limited opportunities for successful reproduction, especially during periods of drought or low water levels.

In extreme cases, where absolutely no facilities exist for viable spawning, a trout fishery

Q & A

What makes a good trout water?
The very best trout streams and lakes offer cool, relatively clean water with deep enough holes to offer protection for the fish even during a drought. Ideally, they are spring or snow-fed, or have their headwaters in a cool alpine or sub-alpine area that lies at least 1000 metres above sea level (this is less important in Tasmania, with its colder climate). Finally, a good trout water will hold abundant food in the form of insects, insect larvae and small fish. All of these food sources are normally associated with weed beds, sunken or drowned timber, gravel or rock beds and healthy bankside vegetation.

How big do Australian trout grow?
In most waters, any trout topping 2 kg is a good fish and specimens much over 3 kg could be classed as exceptional. However, newly-filled lakes and dams may produce outsized trout because of the incredible abundance of food and lack of competition. Examples were Eucumbene and Jindabyne (New South Wales) in the 1960s, Peddar (Tasmania) in the 1970s and Pejar (New South Wales) in the early 1980s. Impoundments such as these turn up the occasional monster fish in the 7 to 10 kg range, though it's worth remembering that the maximum growth potential for both brown and rainbow trout in their home waters (Europe and North America) is closer to 18 kg!

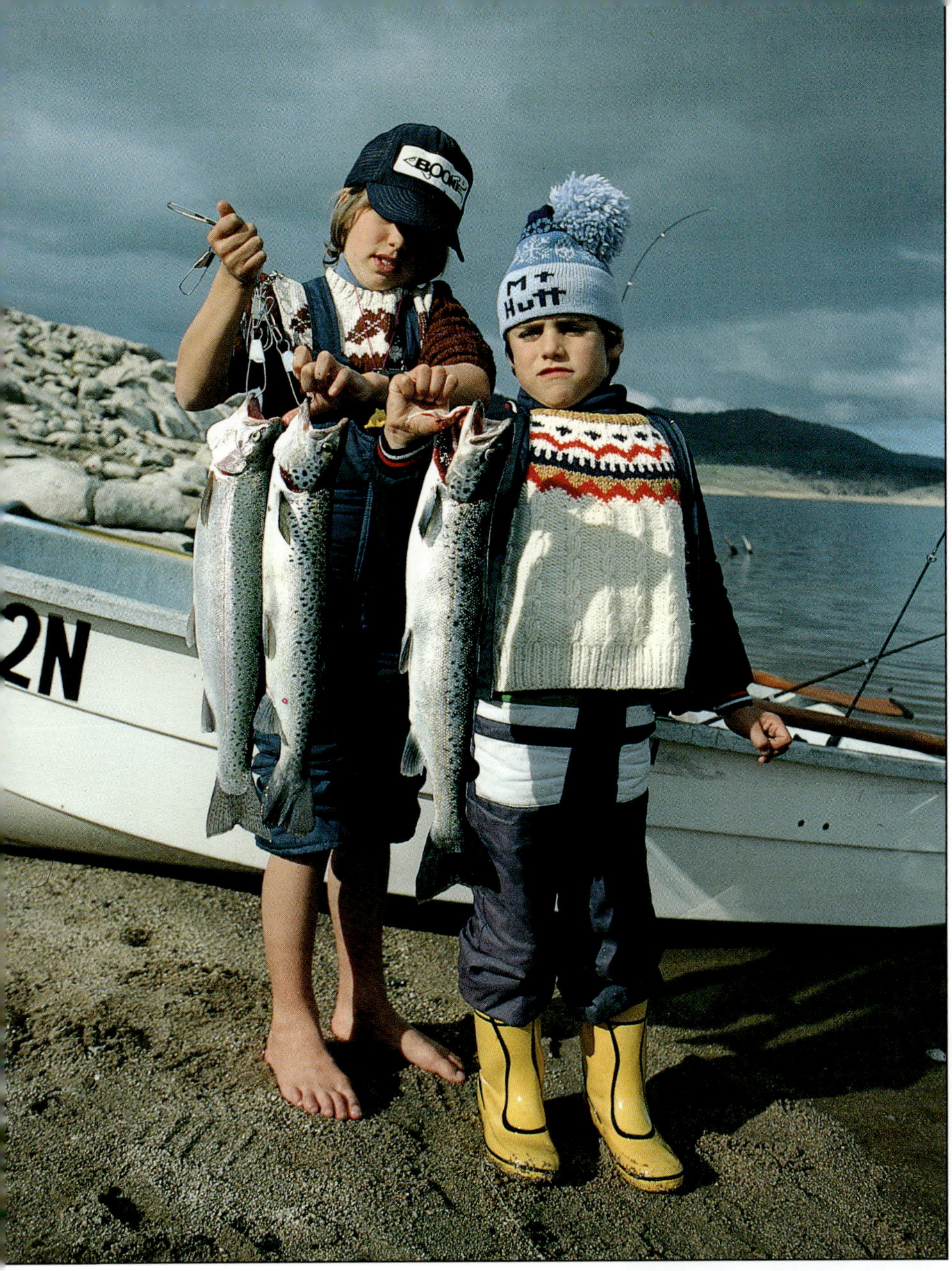

LEFT: You're never too young to begin trout fishing! Here the catch consists of a rainbow (left), a brown (centre) and a landlocked Atlantic salmon, all taken from Lake Jindabyne in the Snowy Mountains.
BELOW: Approximate trout distribution in Australia.

may only be maintained on a 'put-and-take' basis, with every fish caught being the product of hatchery work. On the whole, such put-and-take fisheries do not represent a good return on capital outlay and are gradually being replaced with native fisheries based on species such as golden perch, Murray cod and catfish. Copeton Dam near Inverell and Glenbawn Dam in the upper Hunter Valley (both in New South Wales) are good examples of such rationalisation by fisheries management authorities.

At the opposite extreme, Australia does boast some superb, self-sustaining trout fisheries. The best of these are represented by the many upland streams and lakes of Tasmania, although fine populations of 'wild' trout, particularly browns, also occur in the alpine regions of Victoria, New South Wales and the Australian Capital Territory. The browns of Lake Eucumbene, in the Snowy Mountains region of New South Wales, are a perfect example, having proven so successful that they now compete with stocked rainbows to the detriment of the latter species.

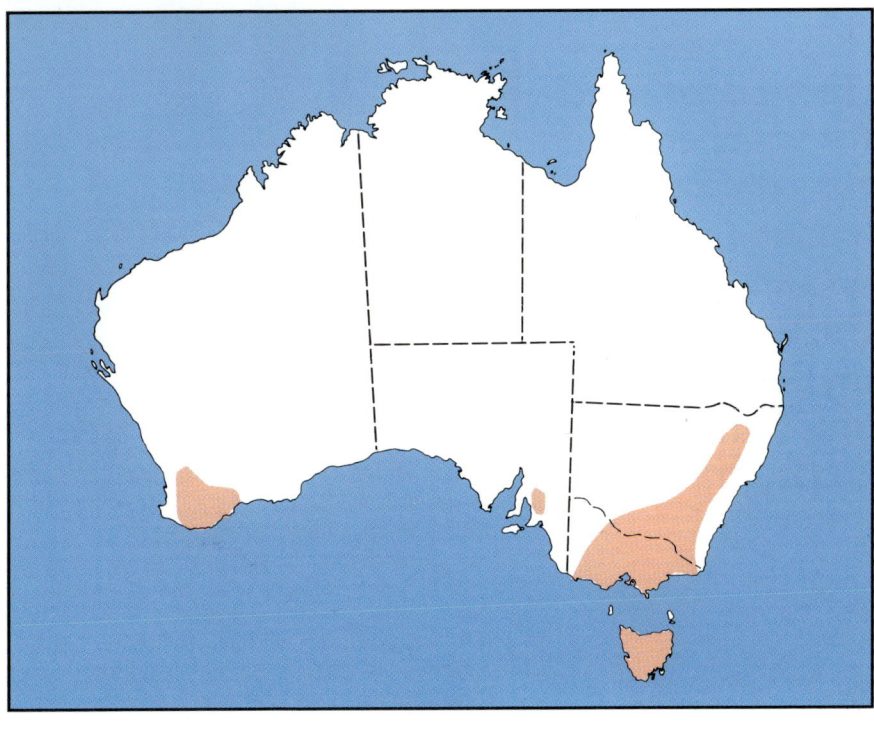

ABOVE: A fat rainbow flanked by two fine browns.

RIGHT: A trio of rainbow trout taken while trolling in Wyangla Dam, western New South Wales.

'There is no need for snobbery or class distinctions among trout anglers, nor is there anything mystical about any form of trout fishing.'

Fishing for Trout

Trout fishing is undoubtedly the most popular form of inland angling throughout the southern half of the continent, attracting tens of thousands of devotees each year. Levels of skill and expectations vary immensely within the ranks of trout anglers, but all share a regard for the great outdoors, a love of the peace and solitude offered by trout fishing and, above all else, a passion to match wits with these attractive and tasty adversaries.

Trout may be fished for using a wide variety of tackle and techniques. They respond well to the careful presentation of baits such as earthworms, insects, shrimp and small live or dead fish. They will also actively attack small to medium artificials (lures), including spinners, spoons, jigs, plugs and minnows. Of course, trout are also the primary target of the freshwater fly fisherman, who uses artificial flies of fur, feather and tinsel presented on specialised tackle to imitate the insects, insect larvae and other organisms which make up so much of the trout's diet.

No Distinctions

None of these techniques or approaches is intrinsically 'better' or more noble than the others, despite the fact that fly fishing is often afforded a degree of reverence based on its rich history and supposed mystique. It should be remembered that most good fly fishers began chasing trout with baits or lures, and will occasionally return to those methods when conditions suit.

There is no need for snobbery or class distinctions among trout anglers, nor is there anything particularly mystical about any of the forms of fishing described, all are easily mastered by anyone with a little patience. It should be noted, however, that gear and technique restrictions do apply on certain waters or at certain times. See box on Trout Fishing and the Law.

The first step towards becoming a trout angler is to select a suitable rod and reel combination or outfit, ideally one which will allow you to pursue several angling styles in a range of locations.

LEFT: A pair of fly fishermen using special wading sticks for support in a swift flowing stream. Although venerated in popular fishing literature, fly casting is just another technique of angling and should not be regarded as superior to bait fishing, spinning or trolling. Each method has its day.

COOK'S CORNER

Trout is an excellent all-round fish. Grilled, poached, fried or baked it is delicious. To poach, simply simmer your catch in water with some parsley, slices of lemon, onion rings, herbs and a generous dollop of white wine, or, cook your catch gently in butter. Follow the recipes for gourmet results or improvise around the campfire for an equally memorable meal.

Trout with Almonds

Trout Cooked in Butter

This is a simple, classic way of preparing trout. The fresher the fish, the better it tastes.

4 x 250 gram trout, gutted,
    scaled and cleaned
185 grams unsalted butter
salt and pepper
1/2 cup flour
juice of 1 lemon
1 tablespoon chopped parsley
1 lemon, sliced

Wipe trout with a damp cloth. Heat butter in a pan until hot. Remove from the heat and allow to stand until milk solids settle to base of pan. Carefully pour clarified butter into another container, leaving milk solids behind.

Season flour with salt and pepper. Place trout in flour and roll to coat it. Pat off excess flour.

Heat 90 grams of clarified butter in a frying pan and when hot add fish. Cook for approximately 10 minutes, turning after 5 minutes, or until cooked. Drain fish and keep warm on a serving dish. Pour cooking butter from pan and wipe clean.

Heat remaining butter in pan until it becomes nut brown. Do not burn. Take off the heat, add lemon juice and parsley and pour over fish. Garnish with lemon slices and serve with new potatoes and spinach.

Serves 4

Trout with Almonds

4 trout, gutted
salt and pepper
1/3 cup flour
90 grams butter
4 tablespoons oil
20 grams butter
60 grams flaked almonds
lemon slices, to garnish

Wipe fish with a damp cloth. Season flour with salt and pepper. Dip fish in seasoned flour and pat off excess.

Heat butter and oil in a frying pan and fry trout on both sides until cooked, about 7 to 10 minutes depending on thickness. Remove to a serving plate and keep warm.

Clean frying pan and heat 20 grams butter. Add almonds and cook until golden. Sprinkle over trout and garnish with lemon slices.

Serves 4

TROUT 2

To Catch a Trout

You don't need heaps of sophisticated and specialised tackle in order to catch trout. In fact, you can even modify your light saltwater and estuary gear to suit!

Gear for trout fishing need not be elaborate and expensive, although many devotees of the sport do ultimately graduate to a level where the best in gear is demanded and, perhaps, justified.

It's possible to buy a very workable trout fishing outfit, including rod, reel, line and basic terminal tackle items for a total outlay of approximately $150. Better still, saltwater bream and whiting gear is usually readily adaptable to trout fishing.

Most of the trout caught in Australia are taken on light fibreglass rods measuring close to 2 metres in length. These are usually matched with small threadline or spinning reels and lines of 2 to 5 kg breaking strain. A set-up such as this is suitable for trolling from a boat, spinning from the bank or casting baits. Add a bubble float for casting weight and you can even fly fish with it.

A closed-face or spincaster reel will readily replace the standard threadline, though this style of reel is not overly popular in Australia. Easy to use and very accurate when it comes to casting, closed-face reels do have certain drawbacks. Foremost among these are limits on the ability to cast ultra light weights, generally inferior drag systems and some increased risk of corrosion because of the enclosed spool design.

Baitcaster or plug tackle built around a small level-wind overhead and a pistol grip rod represents a very enjoyable way of trout

OPPOSITE: Reaching for a beaten rainbow trout taken on fly tackle in a bay on Lake Eucumbene in the Snowy Mountains.
ABOVE: A beautifully marked hen rainbow and the red and black Matuka fly which proved her undoing.
LEFT: One short of a bag limit — and what a bag! These fish fell to a Rapala minnow in customised colours.

'Gear for trout fishing need not be elaborate and expensive.'

Mature male brown.

fishing, particularly when trolling or casting relatively heavy lures and baits. However, only a real expert could hope to cast weights lighter than about 7 grams off a baitcaster, particularly in adverse conditions such as strong wind and cold weather.

Fly Fishing

Fly fishing tackle is quite different from the more conventional gear described above. It is used to cast and present an almost weightless artificial fly. To achieve this feat, casting weight is provided by a special length of thick, relatively heavy line called fly line. A 2 to 4 metre length of fine nylon leader is attached to the working end of this fly line in order to avoid scaring the trout, and in some cases some more nylon or multifilament line is tied on behind the 30 metre length of fly line to facilitate the fighting of a really big fish.

Fly tackle is rated according to the weight of line it is matched to. This line weight number is often preceded by the letters AFTMA, which stand for the American Fishing Tackle Manufacturers' Association, a body which helped set the original fly tackle guidelines.

Most fly tackle used on Australian trout streams and lakes ranges from the ultra light AFTMA No 4 category on up to the medium heavy No 9 weight. By far the majority of outfits in use are No 6 and No 7 in weight. Future issues will contain much more detailed information on fly tackle and fly fishing.

TROUT SPAWNING AREAS

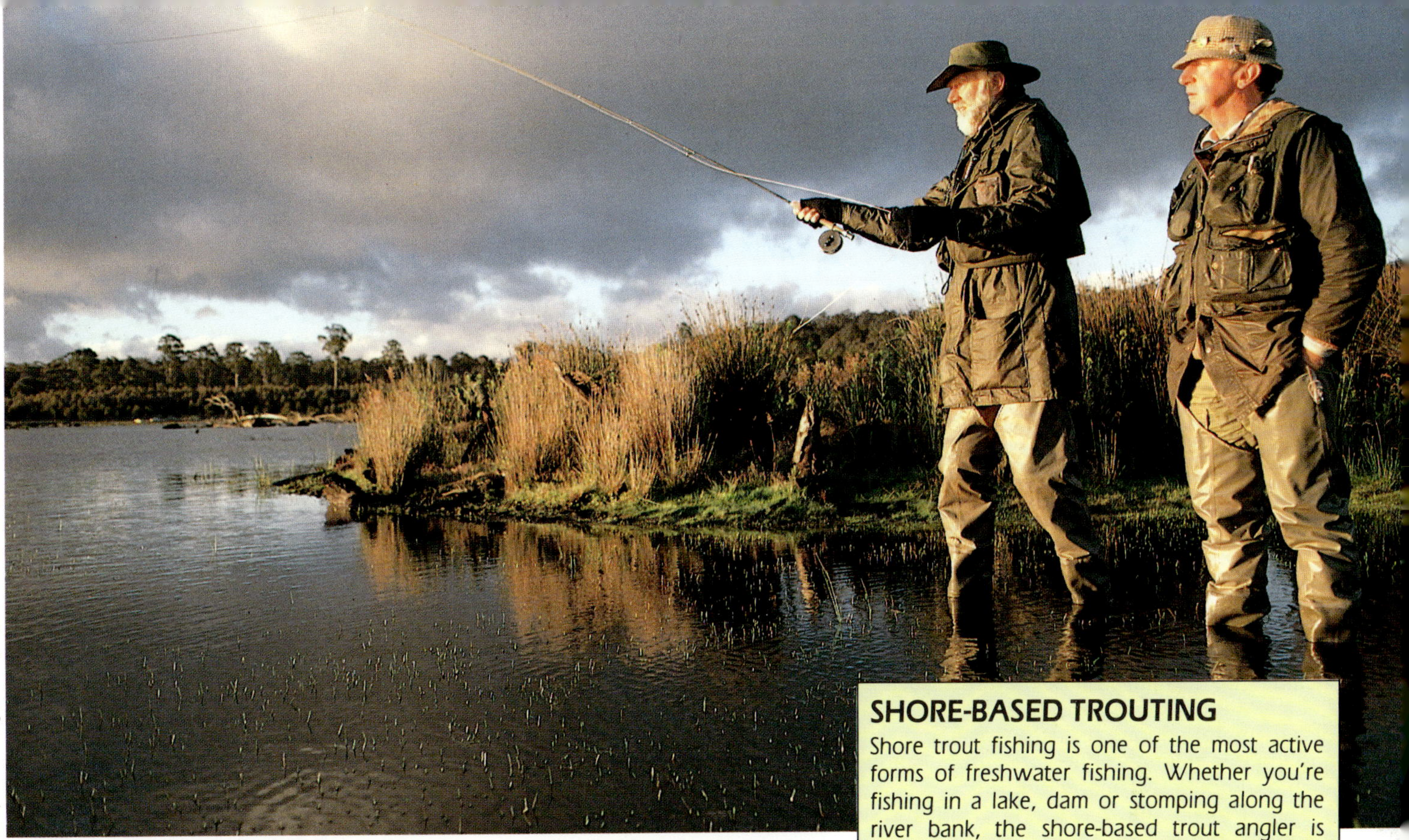

Carolyn Johns / Wildlight Photo Agency

SHORE-BASED TROUTING

Shore trout fishing is one of the most active forms of freshwater fishing. Whether you're fishing in a lake, dam or stomping along the river bank, the shore-based trout angler is always on the move and must be equipped with a supply of lures, hooks, bait and other necessary fishing items.

One of the most compact ways of carrying this tackle is in a fly vest. These pieces of apparel contain a seemingly endless array of pockets and usually include one large enough to store fish. A fishing vest permits the angler complete mobility while carrying the stock of necessary tackle and will prove invaluable for shore-based fishing.

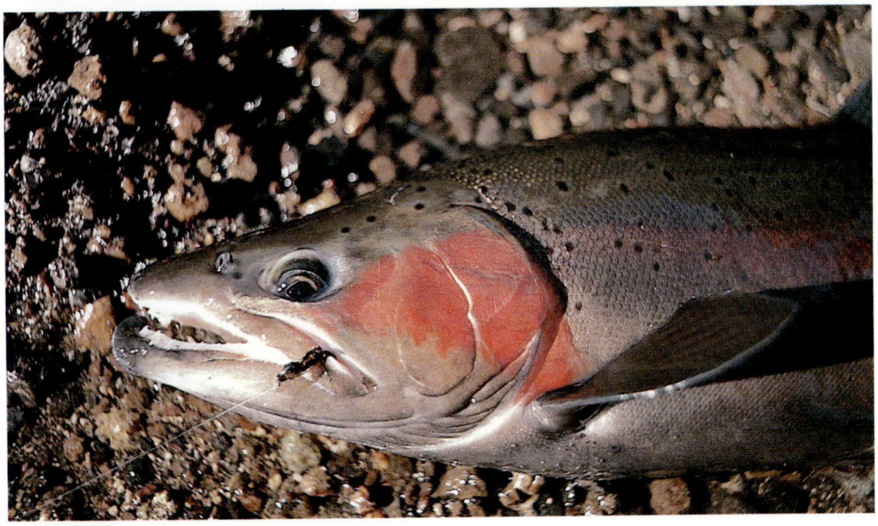

TOP: Fishing the evening hatch.
LEFT: Male rainbow in spawning livery.
OPPOSITE: Baitcaster tackle is fine for trout trolling. This land-locked Atlantic salmon was taken from Lake Jindabyne on a fly trolled behind lead core line.

HOLDING AREAS FOR TROUT IN A TYPICAL STREAM

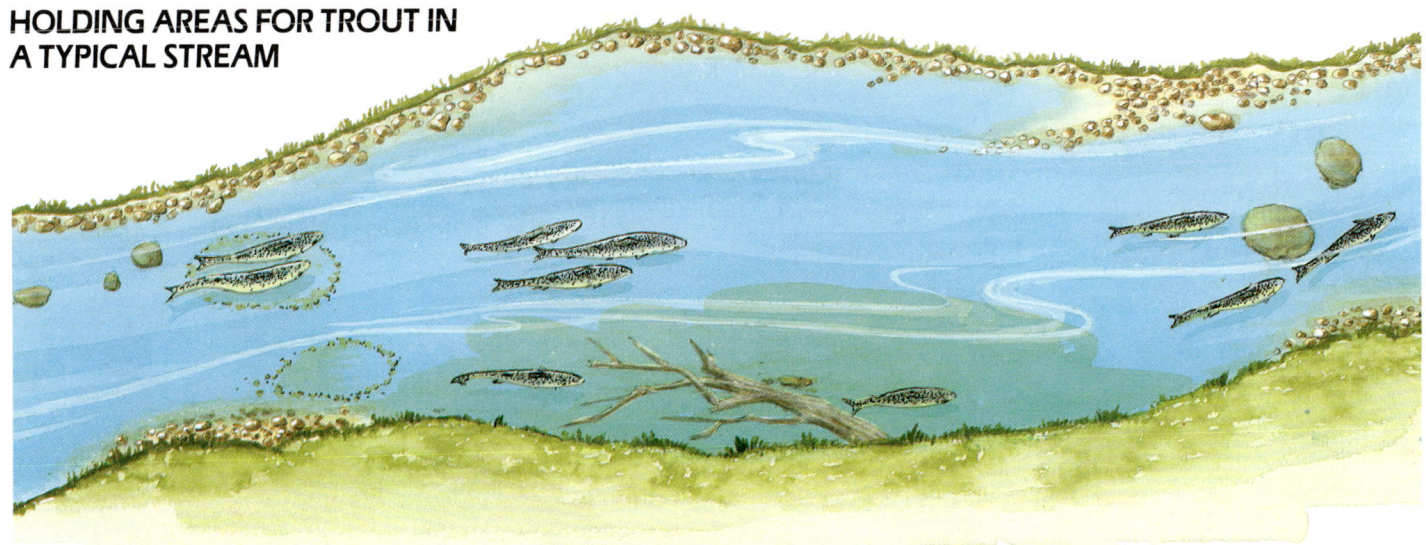

Mature female brown.

Lures and Flies

An incredible diversity of artificial lures and flies appeal to trout at different times, but in reality the angler need only carry a small selection to cover most situations.

Popular trout lures fall into two classes: those mainly used when trolling and those employed in casting and retrieving. Of course, there is no reason why the two styles cannot be interchanged.

Famous and time proven casting lures include the spinning blade patterns such as Celtas, Mepps, Vibrax and the like, as well as dished metal spoons and the smaller plastic and timber minnow-style lures from stables such as Rapala, Nilsmater and Rebel.

Top trolling lures include Flatfish-style wobblers, the Australian-made baltic Minnow, as well as the spoons and bibbed minnows mentioned above. Spinning blade lures may also be used, though ideally in conjunction with specially designed anti-kink keels to reduce the line twist problems inherent with these artificials.

Many Choices

Fly casters are faced with an even more bewildering array of choices, and many keen fly fishermen become fascinated with designing and tying their own special patterns.

Flies fall into three broad groups. Dry flies float on the surface to imitate insects, nymphs are suspended below the surface to represent hatching insect larvae or other aquatic life forms, and wets of one type or another vaguely impersonate a wide range of items which appeal to feeding trout.

Odds and Ends

Many trout anglers use a landing net to aid in the capture of hooked fish. Such devices are almost mandatory when trout are taken from boats, though keen bank anglers often get by perfectly well by sliding or even kicking their quarry ashore after it has been fought and played into the shallows.

Wading trout anglers find thigh boots or chest waders particularly handy. These plastic or rubberised garments keep the fisherman dry and warm and allow him to ford streams and lake backwaters or wade out to reach more distant fish not accessible from the bank.

A hat and pair of polarised sunglasses are invaluable for all trout fishing, particularly on bright or glary days. The combination of hat and glasses allows the angler to see into the water and spot likely fish holding areas, snags, drop offs and even the trout themselves. Sunglasses and a hat offer the additional benefits of reduced eyestrain and protection from sunburn.

Q & A

What is a bubble float?
Made of soft rubber or rigid plastic, a bubble float is an egg-shaped or spherical device fitted with one or more holes enabling it to be partially filled with water. Once weighted with water the bubble allows very light baits and even flies to be cast off conventional tackle, and also acts as a float to suspend the bait and keep the line clear of obstructions.

How strong should the line be?
For trout fishing, lines of between 2 and 5 kg breaking strain are ample, with 3 kg being a good standard.

> 'Wading trout anglers find thigh boots or chest waders particularly handy.'

RIGHT: A beautiful 3 kg rainbow, taken after dark, fins tiredly just out of net range.
BELOW: Fly fishing on a beautiful mountain stream.

Oliver Strewe/Wildlight Photo Agency

> 'An incredible diversity of artificial lures and flies appeals to trout.'

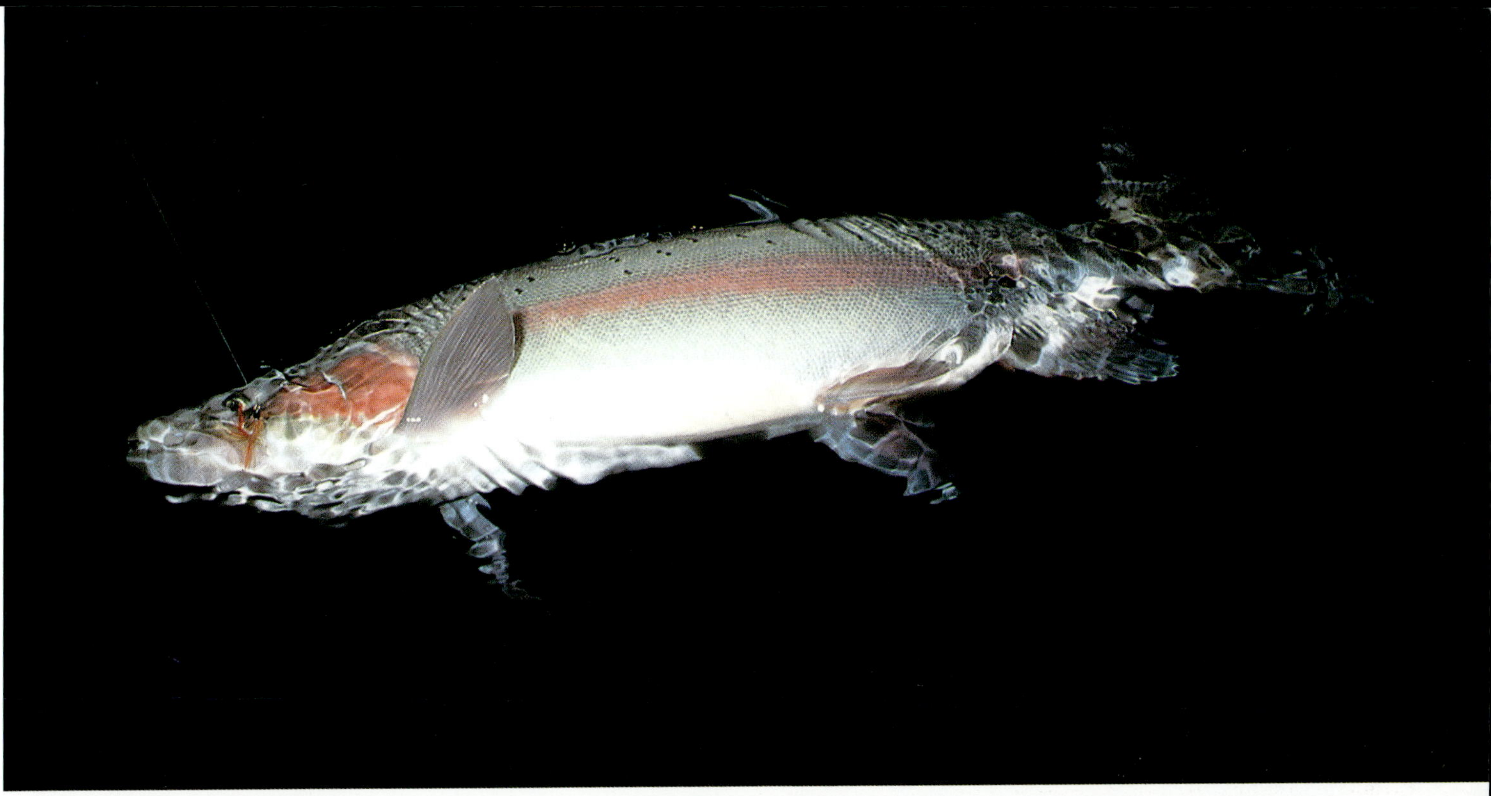

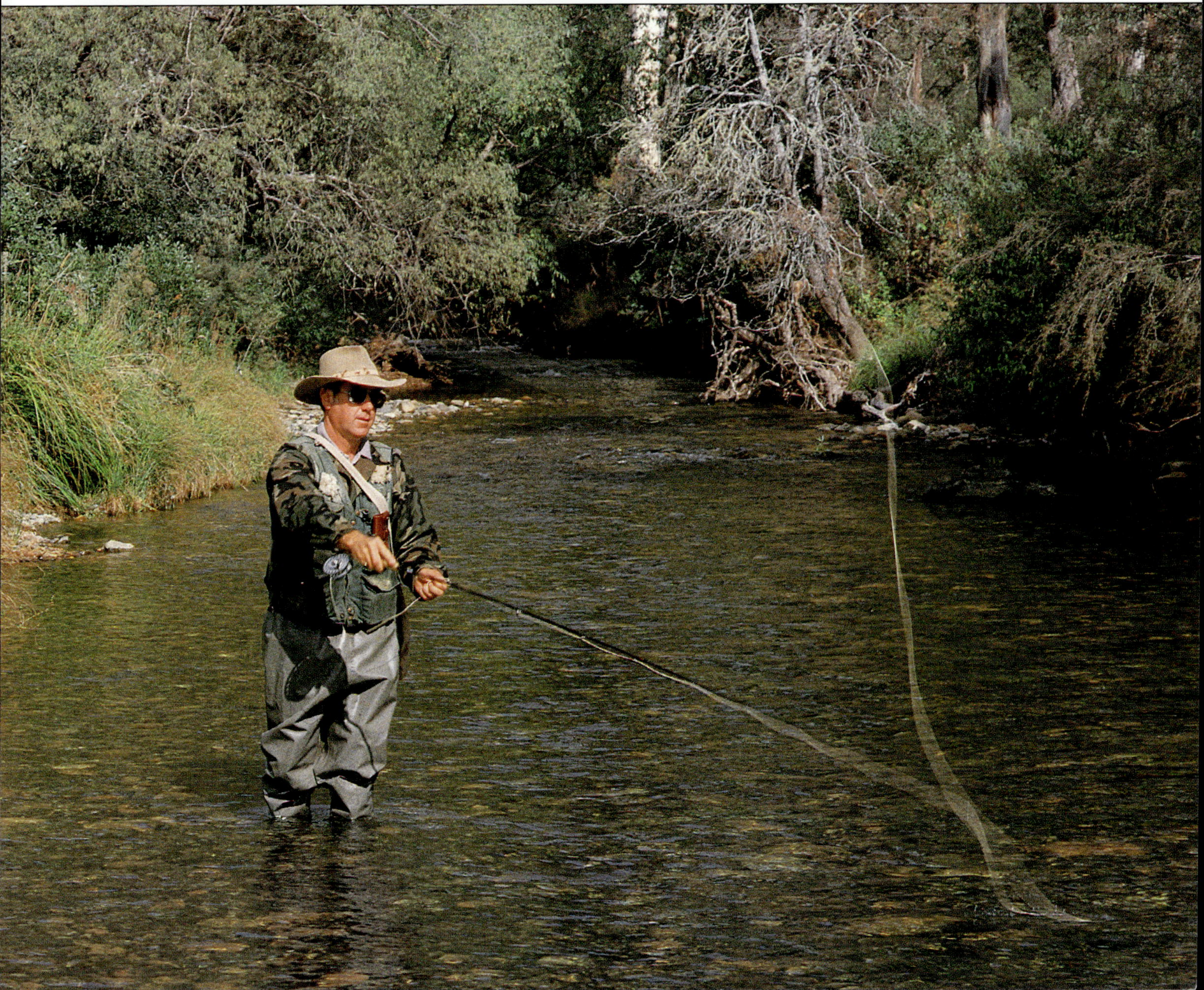

AUSTRALIAN BASS

The ABC of Australian Bass

The Australian bass is surrounded by mystique and legend, based largely on its ability to strike lures and flies with a ferocity out of all proportion to its size. While the fight is usually only short-lived, it is often tense and dramatic if the fish burrows its way into snags or weedbeds . . . A bonus attraction of bass fishing is that it's usually done in some very pretty country.

Ideal bass water can be large or small rivers, creeks, swamps or marshes, but it's usually relatively deep and clean, with a moderate flow and good bankside shade. It should also have clear downstream access to salt water — such as an estuary — so the bass can travel there each autumn or winter to spawn, and mostly it must support a wide variety of prey, such as crustaceans, small fish and aquatic and waterside insect life on which the bass can feed.

That qualifies most of the coastal strip of country from southern Queensland right through New South Wales to northern Victoria as potential bass water. This comprises the modern day range of the bass, though it is extended in the south and west by the range of the very closely related estuary perch, which is found from northern New South Wales to western Victoria and northern Tasmania.

A Fly in the Ointment

Before you rush off and flog all manner of water for little result, you need to grasp that

industry, agriculture and urbanisation have combined over the years to reduce the amount and degrade the quality of available bass habitat.

Pollution has poisoned the water, siltation has reduced the depth and lowered the oxygen content and the construction of innumerable weirs, dams and causeways has contributed to reduced bass stocks by impeding both their downstream movement to breed in the salt water, and their upstream return to their summer feeding grounds.

All that is not meant to depress you, though it well might, but to help you understand what a rare, fragile and precious thing unspoiled bass habitat has become. In angling terms, this means you generally have to travel for your bass, and generally, the more isolated a place, the better the bass fishing.

OPPOSITE: Fins erect and sharp eyes swivelling to track the smallest movement, a juvenile Australian bass holds station on the edge of the current flow just clear of cover. CENTRE LEFT: This distribution map shows the approximate range of bass and estuary perch. For much of their ranges, these two species overlap; however, estuary perch are rare north of the NSW central coast, while bass do not extend south west much beyond the Gippsland Lakes. BELOW: Aussie bass are a mighty handsome fish, and one of our premier freshwater natives. BOTTOM: Sadly, fish like this kilo-plus female are becoming scarcer with the passage of each year. This one was released to breed again.

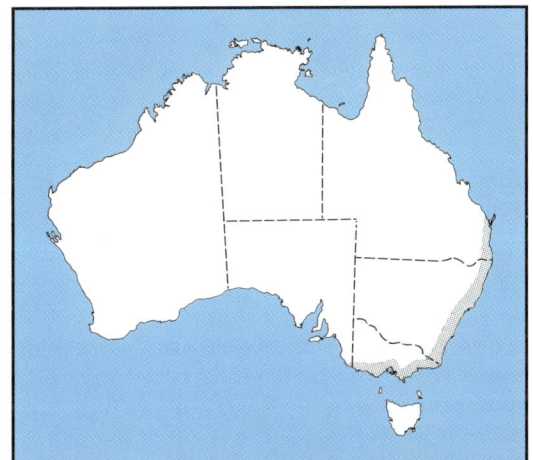

'Ideal bass water must support a wide variety of prey, such as crustaceans, small fish and aquatic and waterside insect life on which the bass can feed.'

BASS AND ESTUARY PERCH

The bass (*Macquaria novemaculeatus*) and the estuary perch (*Macquaria colonorum*) are very closely related. In fact, they have only been separated scientifically in relatively recent times, and most anglers would be hard pressed to tell the difference between them.

Bass range from the Mary River in southern Queensland to about the Gippsland Lakes in Victoria, while perch are found from northern New South Wales to at least the Hopkins, Merri and even the Glenelg Rivers in far western Victoria. It was also once found in northern Tasmania, but it is no longer clear if this Apple Isle population still exists.

As a rule, estuary perch are found further downstream in estuaries than bass, and rarely range much above the upper tidal influence into fresh water. On the other hand, adult bass spend most of the summer well upstream in the freshwater pools and runs of rivers.

Bass and perch differ slightly in overall appearance, though the variations are slight. Generally, perch have slightly deeper bodies, more noticeably 'scooped' foreheads and spinier-looking fin structures. They may also be more silvery in colour, but this is extremely variable. The perch also appears to have slightly larger eyes.

The only good external key for separating bass and estuary perch is the colour of the pelvic fins (the pair of fins under the fish's body just behind the gills). The first ray or leading edge of the bass' pelvics is white or off-white, while the perch's fins are uniformly covered.

When you **do** find quality bass fishing, you soon realise that if you talk freely about it, the thoughtless and greedy may move in and plunder it. As a result, good bass anglers tend to be a tight-lipped group of individuals.

In fact, responsible angling writers have a problem writing about bass. It's a little bit like a drowning man seeking assistance from a group of passing sharks. The more attention you draw to the problem, the worse it gets!

The good news is that intelligently approached, bass fishing **can** survive. In fact, it can even prosper. Moderate fishing pressure alone is rarely enough to deplete the fish stocks of a healthy natural bass fishery. The problem is, as we've said, there's not much of that left. If, however, anglers accept the philosophy of limited kill fishing, that is, voluntary restraint on how many and which fish they kill, the long-term viability of bass angling can be quite good, even in readily accessible locations.

Better Bass Fishing

The equation is a simple one. Bass are under considerable background pressure from reduced and downgraded habitat, and weirs and dams have impaired their ability to recruit new stocks by natural breeding. Therefore, angling pressure needs to be conservative just to maintain stocks, let alone improve them. But it can be done.

The best way to conserve bass stocks and still fish for them is to practise catch and release for the bulk of your catch, only keeping enough fish for your immediate needs.

Single meal fishing is more than just a good way to contribute to the longevity of your sport, it develops your appreciation of the

ABOVE LEFT: Fish intended for release need not even be lifted completely clear of the water.
ABOVE: Night fishing with surface lures is one of the most exciting methods of taking bass — especially lunkers like this 1.5 kg prize. This fish came from the upper Shoalhaven River, an area that is today only a sad reflection of its former self, due to the construction of Tallowa Dam.

'The best way to conserve bass stocks and still fish for them is to practise catch and release.'

value of a single fish, and along the way, it is what prevents angling degenerating into tasteless butchery.

Go ahead, and catch all you like, but only kill what you really need to, and there'll be more and better fish for a long time to come, especially if you keep the right fish.

Which Fish to Keep

Fish population dynamics change with environmental changes, which is another way of saying that what's right for one place now, may not be ideal in five or 10 years time, or in some other area.

Right now, for example — in the late 1980s — scientific research into bass populations conducted in the Nepean-Hawkesbury system by Dr John Harris of State Fisheries, indicates that it's good fish management within this system to keep the smaller male bass, of which there is currently a good supply.

These immature males are nearly all under 25 cm in length. Many of the bass longer than 25 cm will be sexually mature females, and as such, represent the breeding stock vital to the bass's survival as a species. Releasing these breeders in good condition is a chance for you to do something noble and far-sighted. You're actually giving some bass to the future.

So, as a rule of thumb, stick to keeping just one or two bass between 20 and 30 cm for the table and release all smaller and larger fish.

ABOVE: A rare shot of the Bega River in southern NSW with some water in it! These days this heavily silted waterway only flows in this manner at flood time, and although it once produced an Australian record bass, it would be an optimistic fisherman indeed who set his sights on scoring good bass there today.

RIGHT: A selection of deep-diving bass plugs. Generally speaking, the brighter colours are best in dirty water, while the more natural tones should be employed in clear running streams.

'Releasing these breeders in good condition is a chance for you to do something noble and far-sighted.'

ABOVE: A lure-munching bass is led to the bank for release.

'Each feeding situation will be slightly different, but there are some general types of bass "holes" you can learn to recognise.'

Lures and Techniques

Bass are live feeders, that is, they have a preference for live food, which they ambush, or hunt down and kill. This makes them wonderfully co-operative to lure and fly fishermen. It generally means they take live and dead baits with gusto, too.

The greatest single factor in securing a bass strike, whether on lures, flies, or bait, is to put your offering in the right place. When people ask; "Where can I find bass?", there is an enormous range of 'correct' answers.

The loosest possible correct answer is: "Anywhere between Noosa and Lakes Entrance". The most exact answer may well be: "Five centimetres to the right of that blade of grass . . . or twig . . . or ripple . . . or rock."

The vast amount of detail and alternatives between those two extremes is the whole box and dice of bass fishing, and no one article can cover it all, but we can make a start.

The first thing you need to grasp is that you can set out to learn about bass with some confidence. Bass lore isn't unknowable, or beyond ordinary mortals, any more than are the basics of bream, or whiting, or flathead, or trout, but the knowledge won't come without effort and an understanding of the nature of the beast.

First and foremost, the bass is a territorial creature. That is — aside from those times it travels some distance to spawn — it sets up house in a particular corner of the creek or whatever, and heaven help anything edible (or even inedible) that blunders into that private space.

In order to manipulate the bass's natural strike response, you need to put your lure, fly or bait close enough to gain the fish's attention, then make it behave like something non-threatening and, ideally, edible. Finally, you need to do it when the fish is most likely to be in an aggressive and/or feeding mood.

Taking those requirements in turn, before you can put the lure close enough to the bass to have it struck at — let's call this in the 'strike zone' — you have to have some idea where bass hang out.

Bass like to suspend in dark, deep hidey-holes like creek corners, under bankside tree

roots, in amongst the branches of submerged trees, and alongside dense stands of weed. These features generally occur either right on, or just near a sudden drop-off into a channel or hole of much greater depth, or form part of a general constriction of the current flow where food is concentrated.

Each feeding situation will be slightly different, but there are some general types of bass 'holes' you can learn to recognise, or make an educated guess about.

Pick a Lure

Three things should govern your choice of lure and style of presentation, they are: the fish's prey-expectation, or what it expects to see come past; it's probable suspended position, determined by how close it has to be to the current to grab the said morsel; and the current and wind strength.

All three factors are inter-related; the current strength often determining the water depth and fish's position, and also to some extent the likely kind of prey.

For example, very fast water will tend to push the fish right back deep into cover. It can hold station back here without much effort, and most of its prey will be tumbled about by the current and disoriented enough for the bass to charge out and grab it. Alternatively, the bass will get right down onto the bottom where it can shelter in the eddy of some large obstruction like a rock or log and nab the passing trade from there.

Deep holes usually occur on the outside of river bends, especially those with substantial trees which have held the bank profile against erosion above the water line, but allowed the current to undercut the banks, creating eddies and feeding positions where the bass can shelter from the main current while having a clear view of all the food carried past.

Floating diver lures work well in these situations, particularly those with almost neutral buoyancy. These can be cast well upstream of the hole, made to dive under with a sharp stab of the rod tip, then allowed to drift past the submerged lair, carried much closer to the bass by the current than any straight retrieve could effect.

Many good lures will work here, such as Rebel's Suspend 'R', or any other neutral buoyancy floating divers. A lure type not used as much as they deserve to be are the slowly sinking crankbaits like the Sonics, Heddon's Tiny Tad, and Cotton Cordell's Rattlin' Spots.

Large rocks and fallen trees also create feeding stations for bass, often right on the downstream edge of a sand or mud bar. These are often good places to use small lead-head jigs with feather, bucktail or soft plastic bodies like Mister Twisters.

The lure is cast upstream of the drop-off, then allowed to tumble over the edge before being bounced erratically through the hole. Depending on the extent of submerged foliage, some heavy-bodied bladed lures like Jensen's Insects work well in these situations, too.

ABOVE: Fish the size of this female breeder are extremely rare in most waters nowadays.
TOP RIGHT: Landing a lure well past a snag to allow it to dive to a reasonable depth before drawing level with the fish-holding cover.
ABOVE RIGHT: This Williams River bass took a Tiny Torpedo surface lure.

'$10 lures can disappear like magic while you're developing your technique and honing your reflexes!'

Bass are often found in slowly moving pools, and in particular around the bases of bankside trees, under overhanging grasses and tree branches, alongside sheer rock faces and along the deep-water faces of extensive weedbeds.

Where there is significant sunken timber to fish around, you can use very buoyant, long-bibbed deep divers to effectively fish right through the maze of underwater branches.

Crank the lure down to the timber, and when you feel the bib strike an obstruction, stop the retrieve and allow the lure to float up and over the branch then crank it down to the next one, and so on.

This technique is not for the faint-hearted though, as $10 lures can disappear like magic while you're developing your technique and honing your reflexes.

Surface Lures

At dusk and into the evening, surface lures like Jitterbugs and Crazy Crawlers will draw strikes from bass. Cast them close to any solid timber or rock, as these often draw fish like a magnet.

You'll get more fish by letting the lure sit motionless for a few seconds, then start a slow irregular retrieve with twitches and pauses rather than winding the lure straight in.

Flies can be effective on bass, too, especially the fuzzy, big-bodied kind. Fish these as floaters, much as you would a surface popper, with short sharp tugs to make them bloop and send out small shock waves like a frog or grasshopper swimming.

The Bass Season and Bass Baits

While you can catch them in the spring and autumn, bass are generally best fished for during summer, when the hot, steamy evenings and cool clear mornings promote plenty of insect movement and provide the bass with a good supply of active food items.

In late spring in most freshwater rivers, there is an explosion in the local shrimp population. These can be scooped from weed beds with a fine mesh scoop or gathered in traps baited with bread or laundry soap.

Fish big shrimp on tiny fine wire hooks passed once through the tail, or if the shrimp are really tiny, stick a few at a time onto the hook to make a more substantial bait.

Other than shrimp, baits can be a variety of naturally occurring food items, like crickets, grasshoppers, cicadas, frogs, gudgeons or garden worms.

Fish the insects as surface baits and the worms and gudgeons near the bottom under a float with a tiny split-shot to keep the bait deep.

THE MIGHTY MURRAY COD

The Outback's Greatest Prize!

The largest and most important of Australia's freshwater fish and one of the biggest freshwater species in the world, the Murray cod offers inland anglers some great sport and superb eating.

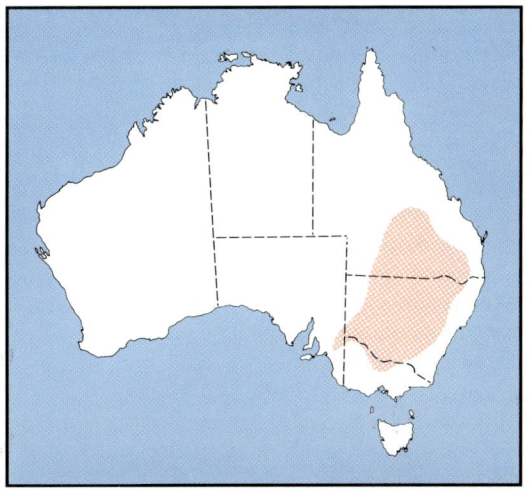

The Murray cod is not related to the true cod — a saltwater fish of the northern hemisphere — but is, in fact, a member of the Serranidae family which includes a number of freshwater perch and the Australian bass.

The Murray cod was once found in nearly all parts of the Murray/Darling River system, which comprises a large number of important rivers in New South Wales, Victoria and Queensland.

In the early years of outback settlement, specimens were taken from many different points and transferred to new locations; mainly dams and other river systems, but also interstate to waters as far away as Albany in Western Australia.

Successful Transplants

Although many transplants failed, a surprising number succeeded. In certain areas, especially some dams on coastal rivers in New South Wales, Murray cod have survived particularly well.

Western dams successfully stocked or re-stocked with the fish include Burrinjuck, at the junction of the Murrumbidgee and Goodradigbee Rivers near the New South Wales town of Yass, Burrendong Dam, which holds back the waters of the Macquarie and Cudgegong Rivers near the town of Wellington, Copeton near Inverell, Glenlyon

west of Tenterfield, several dams in south western Queensland and a number of lakes near Horsham in western Victoria.

Dams in the Sydney catchment region like Warragamba, Prospect, Avon and Cordeaux all have healthy stocks of Murray cod, although unfortunately these impoundments are off-limits to anglers because they form part of the metropolitan water supply system.

Moving the fish from its original habitat has meant that more anglers have the opportunity to fish for them, and it also means that in some waters that are off-limits to fishermen, the cod will be protected and adequate stocks will ensure the survival of viable quantities of brood stock for future breeding programs.

Profile of an Outback Brawler

The Murray cod is a powerfully-built fish with a deep, rounded body. In exceptional instances it grows to a length of nearly 2 metres and weights of 100 kg, although specimens larger than 40 kg are rare these days.

The cod has a large mouth and a big, rounded tail. Its colour is generally creamy-yellow on the flanks with a greenish brown back and pale cream belly. It is covered on the back and sides with mottled dark green to black blotches. The dorsal and caudal fins are covered with dark green spots and markings, and in clearer water the fins display clean, white margins.

OPPOSITE: This shot shows the classic features of a big, bad Murray cod on the prowl.
TOP LEFT: An outback angler nets a nice Murray cod in the Darling, downstream from Bourke.
ABOVE: The traditional cod kill pic' — a pair of monsters dressed and hung on a pole for the family album snapshot. The location is Loxton, SA.

'Moving the fish from its original habitat has meant that more anglers have the opportunity to fish for them.'

The Breeding Cycle

Spawning is usually stimulated by a rise in the water level combined with a rise in water temperature, though it can occur without an increase in water height in some locales. It usually takes place in late spring or early summer.

The fish may move upstream against floodwaters prior to spawning and this upstream movement is well known and eagerly awaited by local cod fanciers along the major inland rivers.

Home Among the Snags

Murray cod occur in some swiftly moving waters, but generally they prefer warm, sluggish sections of a river. They often make their home in the deeper holes where they can take cover in or around hollow logs, among drowned trees and near large, semi-submerged rocks and boulders.

Any natural obstruction to the water flow is a likely Murray cod hang-out.

As well as the obvious snag and log spots, areas close to the outward bends of the river where the current has cut into the clay banks are good for prospecting. These clay banks offer shelter for the fish and are usually loaded with yabbies and other natural foods of the cod.

Murray cod are most active in summer months, especially at night. During daylight they usually shelter near submerged logs or rocks and take up a position where the current and back eddies will bring food to them.

The cod displays lightning fast speeds over close distances, enabling it to catch even quick swimming prey, and also to snap the lines of unwary or inexperienced anglers.

Boating is Best

While it's possible for river bank fishermen to take good catches, for serious fishing a boat is almost mandatory. There are many good, natural landing areas, especially along the Murray, where sandy beaches and launching ramps allow boat anglers to set out along many kilometres of navigable waterways. The same applies on most outback dams.

The choice of boat is important. The craft needs to be easily handled and capable of getting right in among the snags which represent typical cod country.

While anything up to a houseboat can be used on inland rivers and dams, an aluminium dinghy with a small to medium outboard motor is ideal for cod fishing.

Baits and Feeding

Murray cod are voracious eaters and feed on virtually anything smaller than themselves, including other fish, yabbies, shrimps, mussels, water birds, water rats, lizards, frogs, grubs and worms.

Although the spread of European carp through the outback river systems has been regarded by many as a menace, it has provided food for indigenous fish, especially the cod.

'When it decides to bite, it does so with a quick lunge and takes the offering completely into its mouth with a lightning fast movement.'

BELOW: When the water is clear enough to see a pale object held 25 or 30 cm beneath the surface, lure fishing starts to come into its own as a cod catching technique. This 7 kg-plus beauty fell to the charms of a big, deep diving minnow in that classic dirty water colour; bright yellow. This style of lure may be cast or trolled — but always close to cover for best results.

Where it is legal, small live carp make good baits. Another favoured bait is a large, lively tiger or red worm which will take cod up to 3 kg and more.

Many Murray River anglers believe the best bait of all to be the bardie grub; the large, juicy larvae of a giant moth which is found in the ground under the limbs of red gum and yellow box trees along the river banks.

For those not keen on collecting these grubs, supplies can sometimes be bought at local towns near cod fishing waters.

The cod can also be enticed by a bait of shrimp but not many really big specimens are caught this way. On the other hand, a big yabby — crushed to allow a flow of juices — will occasionally attract a large cod.

Frogs are another natural bait for Murray cod; they mostly drop from overhanging trees at night when the big cod are waiting. Frogs can be collected during the day by looking under hanging bark on any tree along the river bank.

Bites on Baits

The bite of the Murray cod is usually easily distinguished from that of the carp, which mainly sucks on the bait.

The cod first peruses a bait, attracted by the smell or vibrations and observes it for a few moments. When it decides to bite, it does so with a quick lunge and takes the offering completely into its mouth with a lightning fast movement and snap of those cavernous jaws. The cod may then turn the bait around in its large mouth before swallowing it, especially if the offering is a live fish.

It is during this second action that the fish

will fall victim to a nicely presented hook. Many anglers miss a Murray cod by not allowing the fish a little slack line after first registering a strike.

If you strike too soon, the hook is likely to miss sinking into the hard mouth parts of the fish. Let the bait go a little deeper and a hook-up is almost assured, for although the cod has a large mouth, it's very much a one-way passage; everything slides in easily but doesn't always come out as readily.

Cod on Lures

The Murray cod is very susceptible to a well chosen and presented lure. Dams and inland lakes are a good spot to try lures on cod, especially through the period between October and May when the fish are particularly active. Working the backwater areas near drowned timber will bring the best results.

Outback rivers also provide fine lure casting and trolling, particularly on those relatively rare occasions when the water runs clear.

The Flopy and Flatfish are two evergreen favourites with cod anglers, though nowadays anglers have a very wide selection of imported and locally produced lure ranges from which to select their cod plugs. These include various Rebels and Cotton Cordells, Storm Hot'N'Tots, Hellbenders, Rapalas, Bennet McGraths, Newells and the like.

As for lure colours, most cod chasers agree that bright fluorescent yellows and reds are best in dirty water, while more natural brown and green hues work best in clearer conditions.

Most cod fishermen who use lures also agree that late in the afternoon until darkness falls is the best time to take the bigger cod, although they can be taken at any time.

Watch the Barometer

Atmospheric pressure can play a big part in hooking a cod, and most regular anglers like the mercury to be quite high. When clouds gather and the weather is building towards a thunderstorm after a hot, still day, cod often turn on a real spurt of activity.

ABOVE: These three photos show the gathering of bardi grubs for use as cod bait. Firstly, a piece of wire is given a corkscrew bend at the end. Next, a likely hole is located by clearing leaf litter at the base of a tree. Finally, the grub is extracted by inserting the wire and twisting it. The result is one of the best outback baits available.
BELOW: Deep diving lures with large bibs or diving lips are best for cod, and bright colours are preferred in the often turbid waters of the outback.

Tackle for Cod

The best cod territory consists of a mass of sunken trees, sharp rocks and other obstacles conducive to broken lines and lost lures. Inland streams can be very hard on tackle and in the course of a day's fishing, it's not unlikely that you'll have to sacrifice a fair amount of terminal tackle.

Six kilo breaking strain line is considered light tackle for a Murray cod in most areas, and if you're after a big one, you'll need 8 kg-plus tackle in the majority of locations.

While more traditional outback anglers may opt for a handline or a set line, modern sportfishermen prefer a baitcaster or medium weight threadline outfit, especially for lure casting and trolling, though the same gear is ideally suited to bait soaking as well.

Accurate Casting

Long casting is not usually required when cod fishing. Accuracy in dropping your bait or lure onto the edge of a likely hole or snag is more important, but beware of the current which will quickly drag your line around and snag it.

On some days, you may need to go from pool to pool along a given stretch of the river or drift from snag to snag if boat fishing. This will increase your chances of taking home a cod. It's often futile to keep casting a bait in one area when the fish are in holes elsewhere.

Set Lining

Fishermen working the western rivers long ago devised a rather unsporting but very effective method of taking Murray cod with set lines. These are usually put in place at night, and baits of live fish, yabbies or grubs are mostly used with the very heavy lines. The

'Although Murray cod fishing may never return to the good old days, recent statistics show that the fish has made something of a comeback.'

BELOW: This beautiful specimen shot shows the clear, striking markings of a Murray cod living in clean, flowing water. Note the distinct white margins on the tail lobes, second dorsal and pelvic fins. Well marked cod like this are common in the New England district of NSW, as well as in some cleaner, southern and outback waters

OPPOSITE: An outback angler poses with his 15 kg cod alongside a typical western river. Judging by the hook in the fish's jaw, it was taken on a heavy-set line rather than the light rod and reel he's holding!

line is then tied to a stake, branch or rubber springer.

Check your local fisheries regulations before setting any lines, as their number and style are likely to be the subject of various rules.

Environmental Factors

Ten years ago there were serious doubts in some circles that the Murray cod would survive as a species. Victims of an altered natural habitat and over-harvesting, cod numbers had dwindled dramatically since the Second World War.

Many rivers, especially those on the western slopes of the dividing range, have become shallowed with siltation and cooled by outflows from deep dams. The introduction of carp, redfin and even trout has combined with this siltation and the building of dams and locks to place extra pressures on fish stocks.

Increased pollution and water regulation to accommodate the growth of towns and agriculture along the Murray River has added to the generally grim picture.

On the positive side, fisheries management authorities have been actively breeding and re-stocking cod in rivers, dams and lakes since the late 1960s.

A Comeback for the Cod?

Although Murray cod fishing may never return to the good old days, recent statistics show that the fish has made something of a comeback and is now at least holding its own, with reasonable to good populations present in many areas.

Experienced inland anglers have recently reported that the stretch of the Murray River from Wodonga through to Echuca is one of

the best locations where there is a viable Murray cod fishery. For those anglers with the right tackle, it's even possible to still land a giant specimen if you have time and patience.

However, because the larger Murray cod are the most important breeders, anglers are encouraged to let the big ones go and keep just one or two fish in the 2 to 6 kg range. These cod taste better than their larger brethren, anyway. Unfortunately, most cod chasers want a really big specimen with the appropriate photo for the album, although an increasing number are realising the thrill and satisfaction that comes from putting a big one back.

Good Eating

Murray cod are rated as one of the best eating freshwater fish in the country. It has a distinctive flavour, a tender flaky flesh and adapts well to a wide variety of fish recipes.

Its firm, white fillets or steaks may be poached, cooked in soup, fried a la Meuniere or coated with crumbs and fried in hot oil. Many prefer smaller fish to be stuffed and baked.

To make the most of the fish's superb flesh quality, kill the cod by cutting its throat with a sharp knife as soon as it's taken from the river. It should then be gutted, cleaned and all blood carefully removed from the spine. Where possible, leave the freshly-caught fish in the refrigerator overnight before skinning.

Because of the layer of fat found between the skin and the flesh of the Murray cod, some people consider the fish too fatty for frying. This can be overcome by removing the unwanted fat. Simply skin the fish and scrape away the fatty layer with a knife. The problem is reduced by eating only smaller, leaner fish and releasing the heavyweights.

COOK'S CORNER

A versatile table fish, Murray cod can be grilled, fried, baked, poached or barbecued. It has a mild taste and firm white flesh. It goes well with rice, Chinese-style vegetables and fruit such as bananas and peaches. Mild flavourings like marjoram, coriander and lemon thyme are recommended.

Murray Cod Fish Flan

1 *small onion, chopped finely*
40 *grams butter*
3 *tomatoes, skinned, chopped and seeded*
1 *precooked pie shell*
2 *hard-boiled eggs*
1 *tablespoon flour*
1½ *cups milk*
1 *cup Murray cod, cooked and flaked*
2 *tablespoons grated cheese*

Cook onion in half the butter until opaque. Add tomatoes and cook until fairly dry. Cool. Spread into pie shell placed on baking sheet. Arrange sliced egg on top. Make a roux from remaining butter with flour, remove from heat and stir in milk. Bring to boil to cook flour. Add flaked fish and season to taste. Pour into pie shell. Sprinkle with grated cheese and bake in the oven at 180°C (350°F) for 30 minutes or until cooked when tested.

Poached Murray Cod

1 *onion, sliced*
1 *carrot, sliced*
1 *lemon, sliced*
1 *bay leaf*
1 *kg Murray cod fillets*
sprig fresh parsley
pinch nutmeg

WHITE SAUCE:

15 *grams butter*
1 *tablespoon flour*
1 *cup milk*
salt and white pepper

Place onion, carrot, lemon and herbs in a saucepan with water to cover. Bring to the boil and simmer 10 minutes. Put cod fillets on top of vegetables and poach 10 minutes. Drain off water and serve with parsley and sauce.

To make the sauce, melt butter in a pan. Add flour and cool, stirring constantly, for 1 minute. Remove from heat, add milk, season with salt and pepper and simmer for 3 minutes. Serve in a sauce jug or pour over your fish.

GOLDEN PERCH

The Ubiquitous Yellowbelly

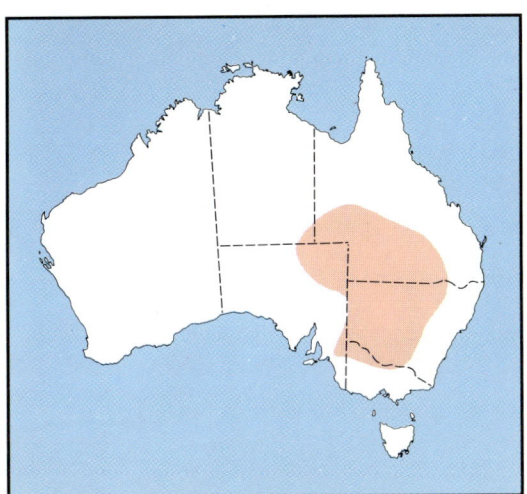

One of the most important fish of our outback and inland rivers, the golden perch — also known as yellowbelly and callop — makes a great contribution to the sport of inland anglers, putting up a good fight, responding to a variety of baits and lures and making an excellent meal.

In an attempt to create some uniformity in fish names, State Fisheries departments have officially given the name of golden perch to the species known by scientists as *Macquaria Ambigua*. However, to those many anglers who fish the waters on the western side of the Great Dividing Range, the golden is more often known as a yellowbelly, callop, Murray perch or white perch.

Golden perch are widely distributed through the Murray/Darling River system, including most dams west of the Great Dividing Range. It is also found in the eastern flowing Dawson River of central Queensland and the Bulloo/Bancannia and Lake Eyre or Coopers Creek drainage systems.

The fish's natural northern limit appears to be the Georgina River which is about halfway between Lake Eyre and the Gulf of Carpentaria. However, as a result of extensive breeding and stocking in recent years, the golden perch has been introduced into many other parts of inland Australia.

Hump Shouldered Predator

Like other species belonging to the same taxonomic group, the golden perch is a deep bodied fish with a solid muscular appearance. Older specimens have a conspicuous lower jaw and the tail wrist is thick, strong and rounded. Males tend to have a more evenly balanced shape and do not grow to the same dimensions as the females which develop a noticeably hump shouldered appearance.

Mature females often appear to have a head that is too small for their body; their body width is often equal to their length from snout to tail. This is particularly apparent in larger specimens.

The golden can grow to weights well in excess of 10 kg, however, most catches these days weigh between 0.5 and 3 kg.

Varied Colouration

The body colour of these fish is usually related to the colour of the waters they inhabit. In the muddy rivers of the plains country of western New South Wales, Queensland and South Australia, golden perch take on a very light cream, yellow or beige colour, with darker spots or mottling.

In clearer waters, the back of the fish may be olive green, lightening to a bluish tinge in fish from semi-clear rivers and dams. Clear water fish sometimes have a crimson tint around the fins, particularly the pectorals. Fish that have lived for some time in clear water develop a deep, golden belly area, but if the turbidity of the water increases, they may lose this colour.

Spawning is influenced by water temperatures and rises in water levels. Fish populations move considerable distances upstream when flooding occurs and spawning takes places when temperatures are between 23° and 26°C.

Spawning usually takes place at night in spring and summer. Larvae swim actively and start feeding on plankton about five days after spawning.

Survival Capacity

Although the golden perch inhabits a variety of river environments, these fish seem to prefer warmer, turbid, sluggish streams. However, the fish have wide physiological tolerances, being able to withstand a range of temperatures from 4° to 37°C! Considering the

'The golden is more often known as a yellowbelly, callop, Murray perch or white perch.'

OPPOSITE: This lovely profile shot of a golden perch shows the species in its glory. Goldens can grow to in excess of 10 kg and fish of this size display a noticeable hump-headed appearance.
BOTTOM LEFT: Golden perch regularly respond to lures when the water is clear, particularly deep-diving plugs like the one that accounted for this fish.
BELOW: Golden perch may change colouration to suit their environment. These two fish display typical variations, although they were taken from the same inland river.

harsh conditions of the Australian inland, these native fish show a remarkable capacity for survival. When the waters dry up during droughts, there are high mortality rates and increased competition for food. However, when the rains finally arrive, the relatively few fish that have survived are able to quickly restore former populations. In a single spawning, a female yellowbelly releases more than half a million eggs.

The Onslaught of 'Civilisation'

In spite of this, the fish have not done well in those areas where fertile soil has resulted in intensive land cultivation. Siltation and pollution due to pesticides are among the major factors which have reduced populations of golden perch.

The main cause of decline through their natural range has been the construction of weirs, reservoirs and locks on the major river systems. These structures impede the natural migration of the fish. Moreover, this regulation of rivers reduces the incidence of flooding, and the lower temperature of water released from these impoundments limits the fish's ability to breed.

The fish have also suffered from sudden fish kills which have been noted in rivers or lakes which have experienced a sudden drop in water temperature. This occurred in the late 1970s when the water in Lake Burley Griffin dropped to 4°C.

ABOVE: When the rivers are in flood, golden perch often make a move upstream to previously inaccessible areas. Here, the scene is the Murray River near Echuca, on the border of NSW and Victoria.
RIGHT: Goldens also respond to bait fishing techniques, although this approach is more often a matter of playing the waiting game as opposed to active lure fishing.

Long Distance Travellers

Tagging has shown that golden perch are able to undertake remarkable long distance migrations.

A fish tagged after being captured from the Murray River below Euston was recovered months later and 350 kilometres away near Leeton.

Another tagged specimen released in the Murray River in South Australia was recovered years later 2000 kilometres upstream in Queensland, in a tributary of the Darling River!

Their migratory pattern seems usually to be upstream and this helps to ensure that there are fish stocks dispersed throughout the habitat range.

One of the top angling spots on the Namoi River is a weir near Manilla. Fish migrating upstream gather at a low rock wall before moving on through a small opening in the rock. At this spot, the fish are often an easy target for local anglers.

'Golden perch are able to undertake remarkable long distance migrations.'

TOP: The Darling River is another recognised producer of golden perch, although one must contend with menacing numbers of carp since their thoughtless introduction into this waterway.
MIDDLE: Landing a golden perch on the banks of the Darling River. A landing net is always helpful for securing goldens at close quarters.
ABOVE: Yabbies can be locally collected at most inland rivers and are one of the top golden perch baits.

'The diet of golden perch consists mainly of crustaceans, aquatic insect larvae and molluscs.'

Sudden releases of cold water from the bottom of dams will push the fish downstream, but when water floods the river from the release of volumes over the spillway, the fish will again move upstream in this flow of comparatively warm water.

Inland fishermen familiar with the fish's movements use local knowledge to take good catches. During spring and summer, many fish leave the dams and head upstream, where they spawn and feed. In the autumn, they often head downstream again to the dam. However, not all fish take part in this migration pattern, and fish can be taken in a well-stocked dam at any time of the year.

Feeding Habits

The diet of golden perch consists mainly of crustaceans, aquatic insect larvae and molluscs. Small fish such as goldfish and European carp also make up part of its diet in some streams. These feeding habits more or less confine them to that part of the water column layers and the bottom or bed of the river.

As far as angling is concerned, the fish can be regarded as a bottom dweller, although it is known that they move into shallow water when feeding at night.

During periods of flooding, the fish will feed on miscellaneous matter that is forced from the ground.

Golden perch have been observed to have two feeding patterns during daylight hours. Some will remain near cover — such as shaded areas, rocks, submerged logs and overhanging shrubs — then quickly move out and take any prey as it passes.

Other fish cruise very slowly over weed beds, sandbanks and pebbly spots and will often burrow their noses into crevices and weedbeds in search of suitable food items. They have also occasionally been seen rising to the surface, almost trout-like, to take live grasshoppers!

As well as this daytime activity, goldens are known to be also active night feeders.

In an aquarium tank, goldens are often seen to feed on yabbies after drawing them into their mouths with a strong, sucking motion from several centimetres away. The yabby was taken both head and tail first, but if taken head first, it was always reversed in the gullet before being swallowed.

Shrimp and Yabby Baits

The most popular baits for yellowbelly include whole yabbies or yabby tails, shrimp, grubs, mudeyes and worms. Baits of live shrimp are a favourite with many inland anglers. These are usually suspended about 30 cm above the bottom fished either under a float or with a dropper or paternoster rig and worked around drowned trees, edges of weedbeds, undercut banks and rocky drop-offs.

Some fishermen prefer to rig their line with a light sinker and place their bait right on the bottom. This technique will take fish but it can also cause snags, as river and lake beds out west can be very rough territory. Often, golden perch choose a certain water depth and remain there in spite of tempting morsels

GOLDEN PERCH STOCKINGS

Public stockings of golden perch in N.S.W. by the Division of Fisheries from 1976 to 1985:

Impoundment or lake	Year of production and No. of fish stocked in thousands										
---	'76	'77	'78	'79	'80	'81	'82	'83	'84	'85	TOTAL
Ariah Park	—	—	—	—	—	—	—	—	2	—	2
Albert	25	—	—	—	28	—	—	—	—	—	53
Ben Chifley	—	—	—	—	23	—	—	—	—	—	23
Blowering	—	—	—	—	251	—	—	146	—	—	397
Burrendong	—	—	180	—	—	—	—	—	22	—	202
Burrinjuck	—	—	35	121	—	—	—	—	—	—	156
Carcoar	—	—	—	—	—	—	—	63	—	—	63
Cargelligo	—	—	—	—	—	—	—	52	—	—	52
Centenary	—	—	—	—	—	21	—	—	—	—	21
Chaffey	—	—	—	—	—	92	—	—	—	—	92
Copeton	—	—	200	—	—	—	—	—	—	—	200
Forbes	—	—	—	—	—	—	—	49	27	—	76
Glenbawn	158	—	—	—	—	—	—	—	—	—	158
Gillenbah	—	—	148	—	—	—	—	—	—	—	148
Hume	—	—	—	—	—	—	181	—	—	—	181
Mulwala	—	—	—	44	129	113	—	—	—	—	286
Pindari	—	—	—	—	92	—	—	—	24	—	116
Urana	—	—	—	—	—	11	—	—	—	—	11
Windamere	—	—	—	—	—	—	—	—	89	—	89
Wyangala	—	—	107	—	—	—	—	—	—	—	107
Wyangan	13	—	—	—	—	—	—	—	20	—	33
Yass	—	—	—	—	26	—	—	—	—	—	26
TOTAL	196	0	670	165	594	237	181	310	184	0	2492

'The typical inland technique of working a lure slow and deep is usually successful.'

ABOVE: Deep diving lures such as these are ideal for targeting yellowbelly, but only when the water is reasonably clear.
BELOW: An angler in the final stages of fighting a large golden perch on the Darling River in western NSW.
BELOW RIGHT: Light spin tackle is ideal for catching goldens. This specimen was taken from the Namoi River in north western NSW, one of the better golden perch hangouts.

placed above or below, so varying depths should be tried until a hookup or two is achieved.

Many fish in inland areas are caught on heavy handlines or set-lines tied to a springer or a branch overhanging the water, and therefore have little opportunity to show their fighting ability under these circumstances. A golden hooked in the mouth on a light line will provide any sport fisherman with a fair tussle.

Another popular technique with baits is 'bobbing'. The bait is bounced up and down on the bottom with the aid of a heavy sinker, the commotion serving to attract them to the bait.

Lures in Clear Water

In relatively clear water, golden perch can be readily taken with a wide range of spinners, spoons and plugs.

The typical inland technique for working a lure slow and deep is usually successful. Casting at areas of logs, rock bars, weed beds and other cover or 'structure' will bring the best results.

Where the water is murky in far western rivers, lures are not widely used as the fish can't easily see or find them. However, a number of deeper holes which have cleared due to long periods of dry weather can often produce fish especially when rain creates a slightly milky flow of water into the pool. Small minnow and yabby-type lures are often successful.

When the water level is really low, the fish are not usually too active. However, when there is a substantial rise in the river level, anglers should concentrate on locations where fish movement is obvious. The junctions of rivers and creeks and those spots which represent a barrier to upstream movement can suddenly become real hot spots.

Unpredictable Biters

Many members of the cod and perch family have the reputation of being 'moody' biters. During one outing they will bite well, but next time out, they can't be tempted. Similarly there will be no action in the morning, then suddenly during the afternoon, one hookup follows the other.

Generally, yellowbelly bite best during spring and autumn and are somewhat sluggish through winter. However, as soon as the river is replenished with fresh rains, these fish will come on the bite.

Baits and lures should be fished fairly deep in the middle of the day and often the best results will be achieved from dusk until a couple of hours after dark.

Anglers will also achieve better results if they adopt a hunter rather than a trapper approach to taking this fish. Lighter lines, lures, flies, sport fishing techniques and a mobile approach will all benefit the angler.

Handle with Care

Golden perch have some physical features than can injure careless fishermen. The spines on the dorsal and anal fins become erect when the fish is taken from the water. A cut from these fins can inflict a painful wound that may become septic if left unattended.

Also, the gill cover has a razor-sharp cutting edge that can badly gash a thumb in the wrong position. To avoid these hazards, the fish should be held upright and its lower jaw clamped between thumb and forefinger. This will keep the fish relatively subdued and allow hooks and lures to be removed without risk of injury.

Firm White Flesh

The golden perch is rated as one of Australia's best-eating, freshwater fish. The flesh is firm,

'The golden perch is rated as one of Australia's best-eating, freshwater fish.'

white and succulent. Larger fish are likely to be lined with fat and as much of this as possible should be trimmed off, particularly along the back line adjacent to the stomach. If the fillets are grilled, the remaining fat will be lost in the cooking process.

If not overcooked, the fish will remain moist and well textured. Like most freshwater fish, golden perch can sometimes have a slightly 'muddy' taint. This is particularly evident in larger specimens taken from turbid waters. However, inland campers are often not fussy and relish a riverside meal of yellowbelly grilled over open coals. Home chefs can overcome this slight taint by the addition of a vghtly spiced sauce to the cooked fish.

Under normal conditions, golden perch keep well and, provided the ice supply is adequate, anglers on extended fishing expeditions will not encounter any problems in bringing home the catch in good condition.

The flesh is excellent for barbecues, smoking, grilling, frying, mornays and sweet-and-sour dishes. The bones are easily removed which makes it a good fish to serve to small children.

COOK'S CORNER
Golden perch is a firm, white-fleshed fish, regarded as one of our tastiest native freshwater species. Larger golden perch tend towards oiliness or fatiness, while specimens from very turbid waters occasionally have a slightly muddy taste. The flesh should not be overpowered with thick sauces. It goes best with parsley, broccoli, asparagus and the like.

Golden Perch with Asparagus

1 small cucumber
2 tablespoons vinaigrette
310 gram can asparagus cuts, drained
375 grams golden perch, poached and flaked
2 teaspoons lemon juice
1 tablespoon chopped shallots
salt and pepper
6 lettuce leaves
6 slices fried bread
3 hard-boiled eggs, sliced

DRESSING
½ cup mayonnaise
½ cup sour cream
1 teaspoon French mustard
2 tablespoons tomato sauce
1 teaspoon dry sherry
few drops Worcestershire sauce
salt and pepper

Slice unpeeled cucumber thinly and marinate in vinaigrette, using either bought salad dressing or homemade (oil and vinegar 2:1 with a dash of mustard and sliced garlic if desired). Combine asparagus, fish, lemon juice, shallots and season to taste. Chill well. Mix dressing ingredients together, chill for 30 minutes. Place one slice fried bread into each of six lettuce-lined serving bowls. Add fish mixture, cover with sauce. Garnish with sliced egg and cucumber slices.
Serves 6

Perch with White Wine

1 kg golden perch fillets
½ cup white wine
½ cup fish stock
2 bay leaves
2 cloves
1 tablespoon chopped parsley
1 white onion, chopped
salt and pepper
20 grams butter
2 tablespoons flour

Place golden perch fillets in a frying pan with white wine and stock to cover. Add bay leaves, cloves, chopped parsley and onion. Season and cover. Simmer until fish is tender, then remove from pan and place on warm serving plate. Strain liquid from pan and reserve.

Melt butter in pan and add flour. Cook until mixture begins to bubble, but not brown. Stirring constantly, slowly add enough strained liquid to make a fairly thick sauce. Pour over fish and garnish with parsley to serve.
Serves 4

Golden Perch with Asparagus.

EUROPEAN CARP

Here to Stay